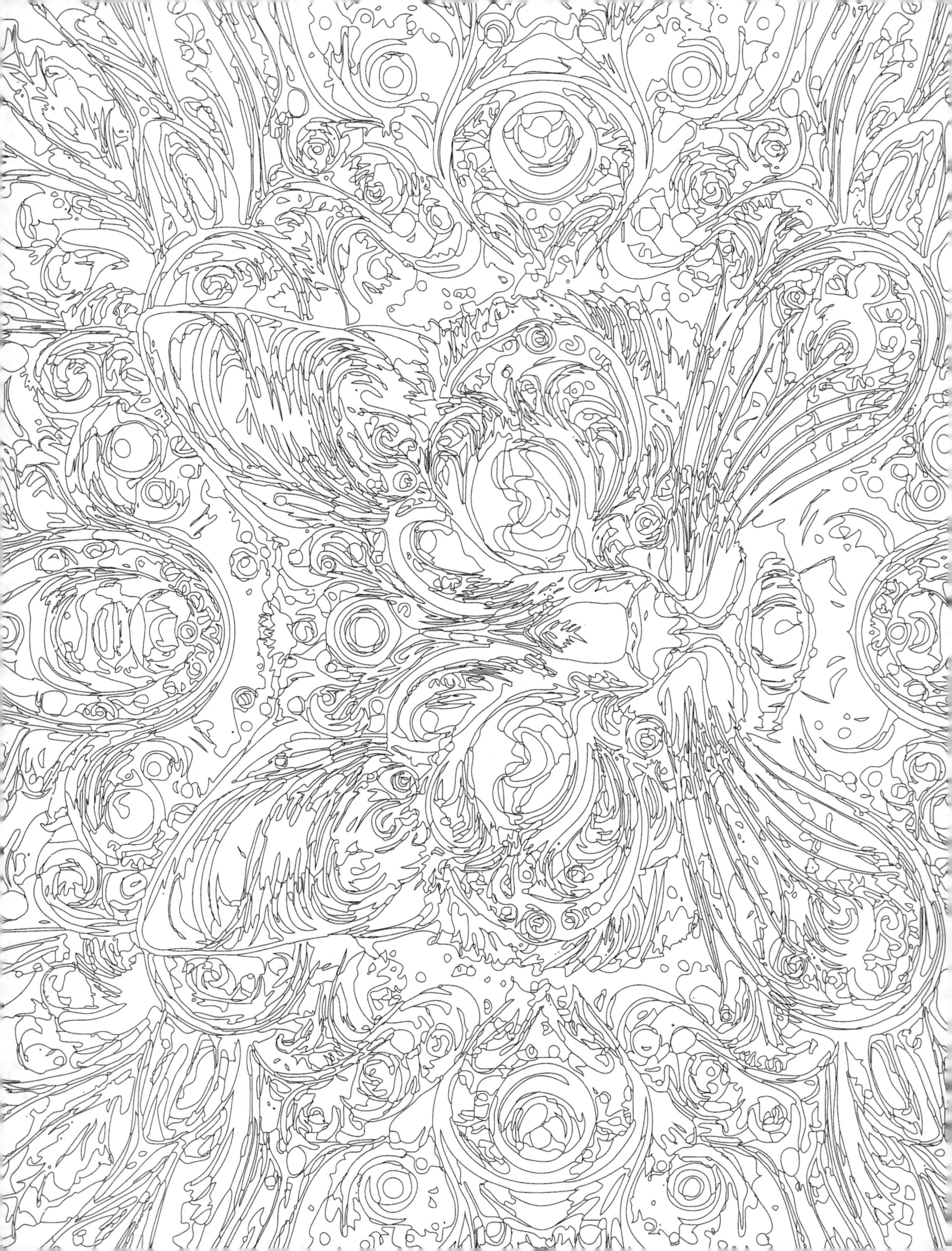

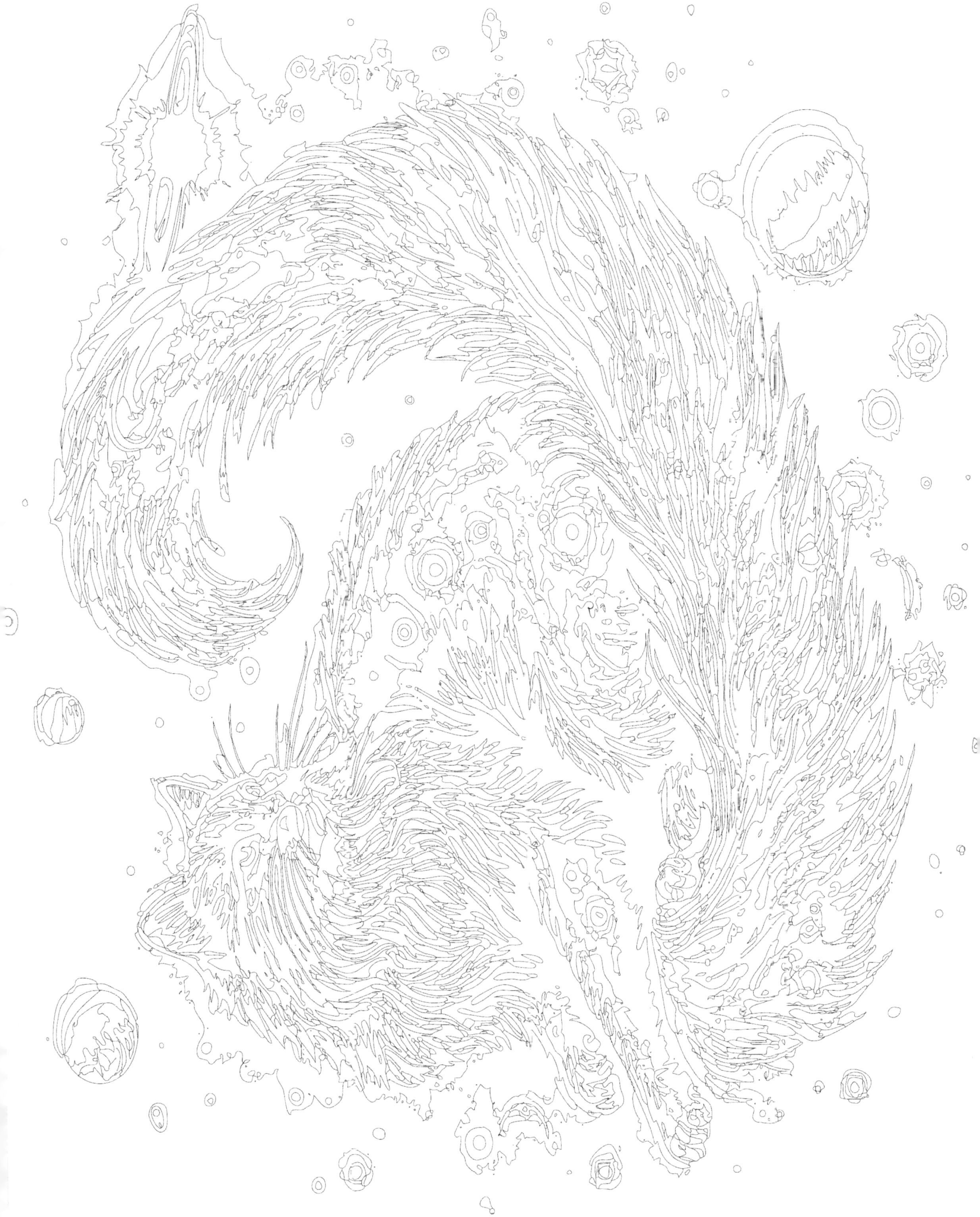

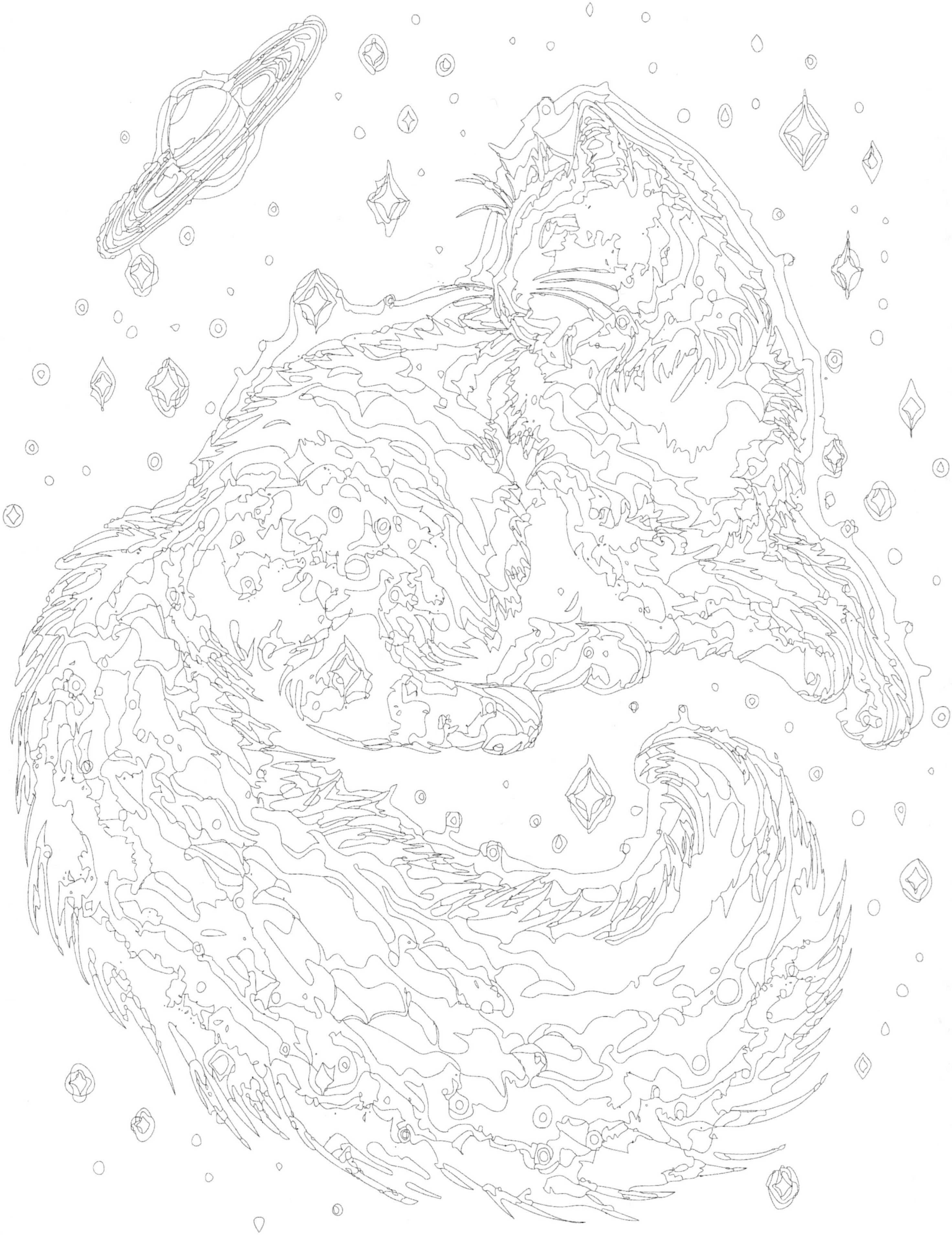

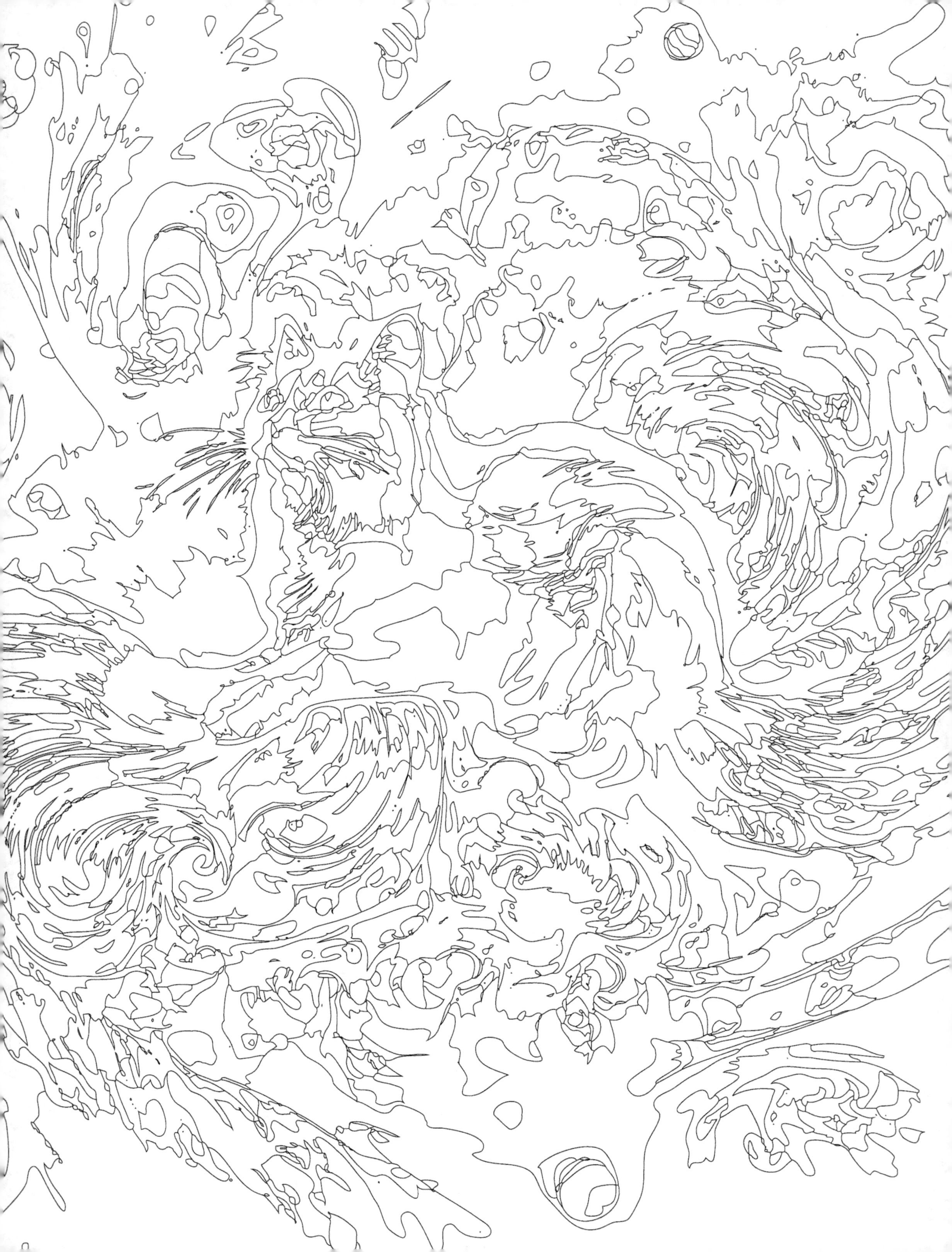

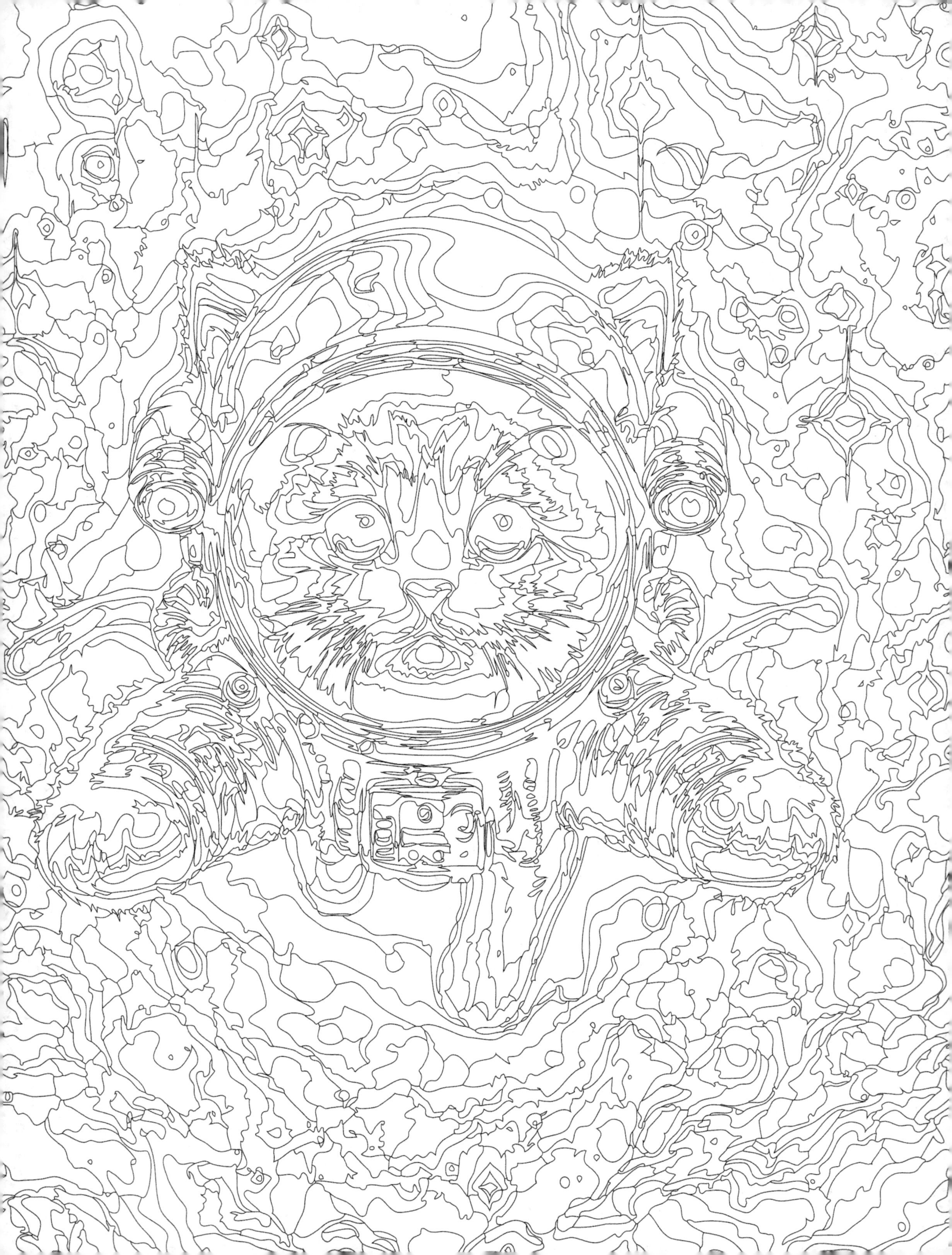

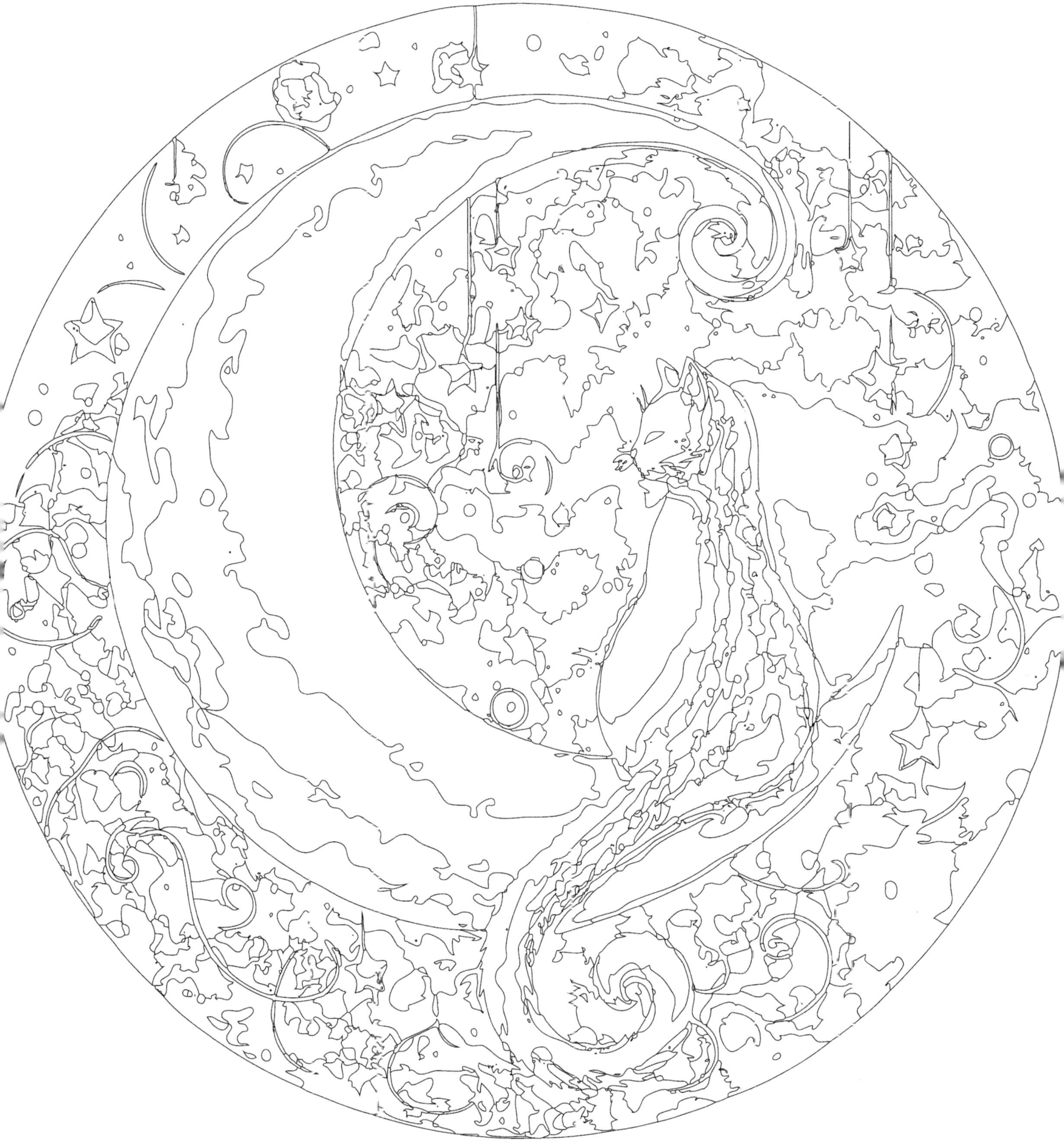

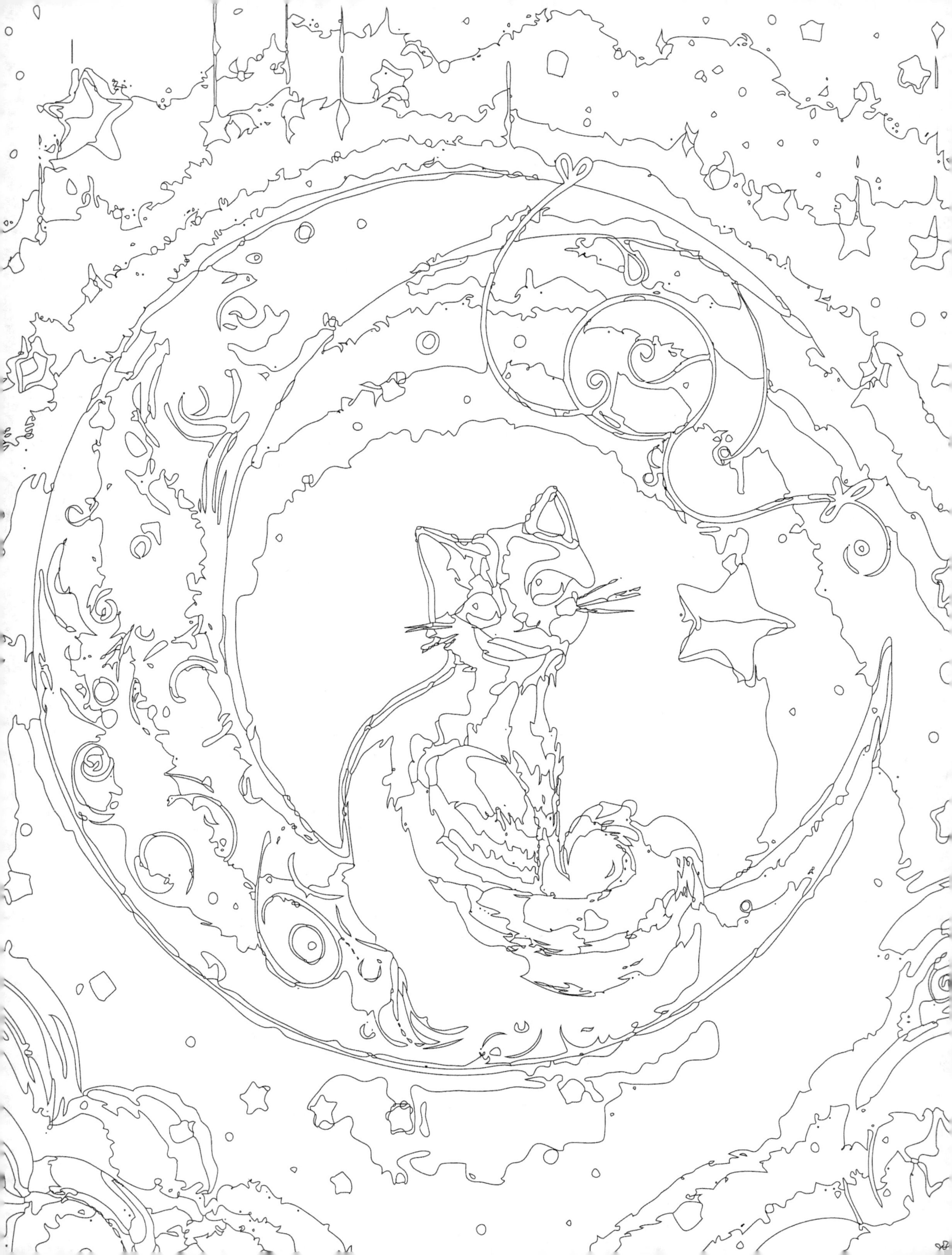

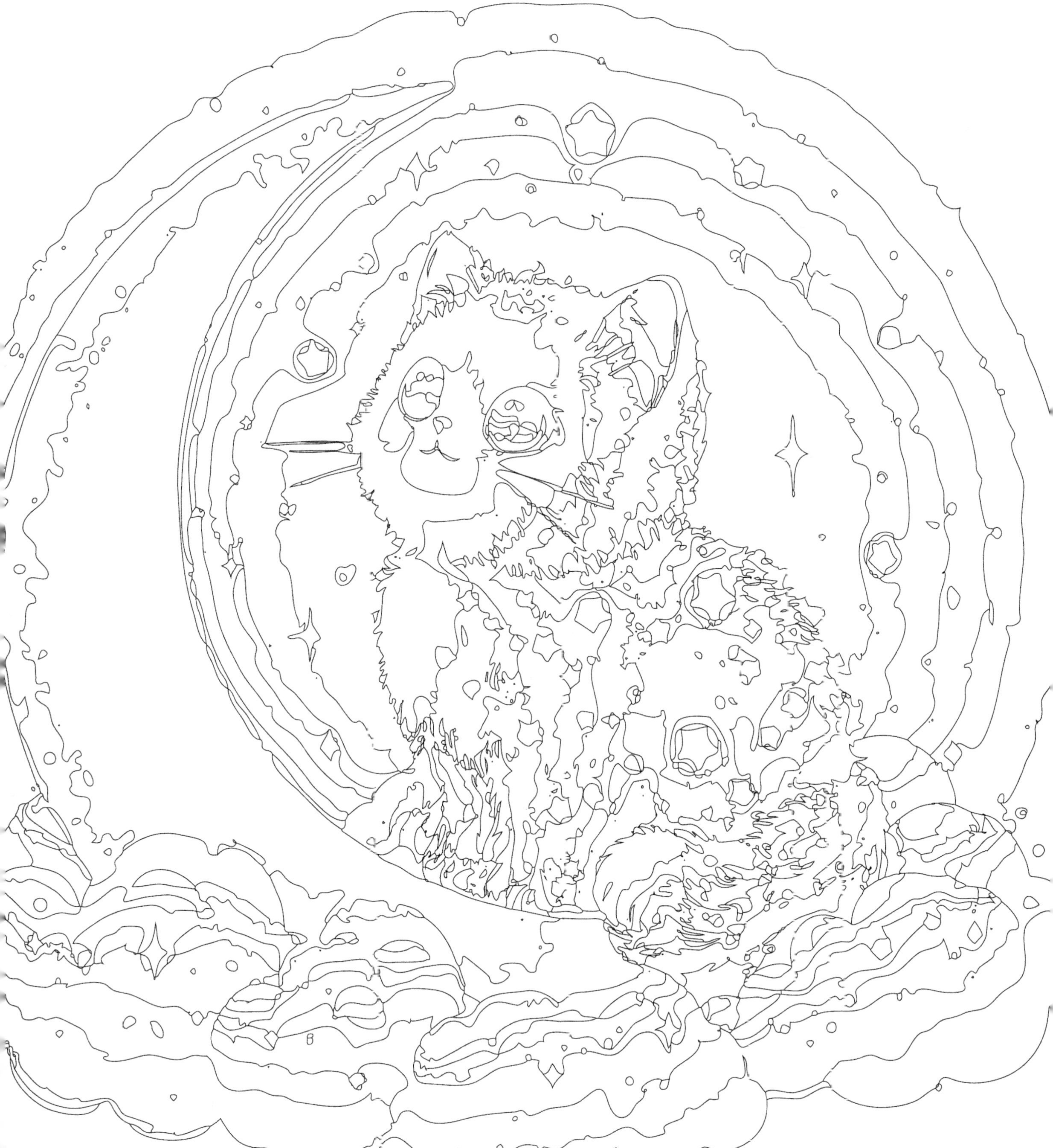

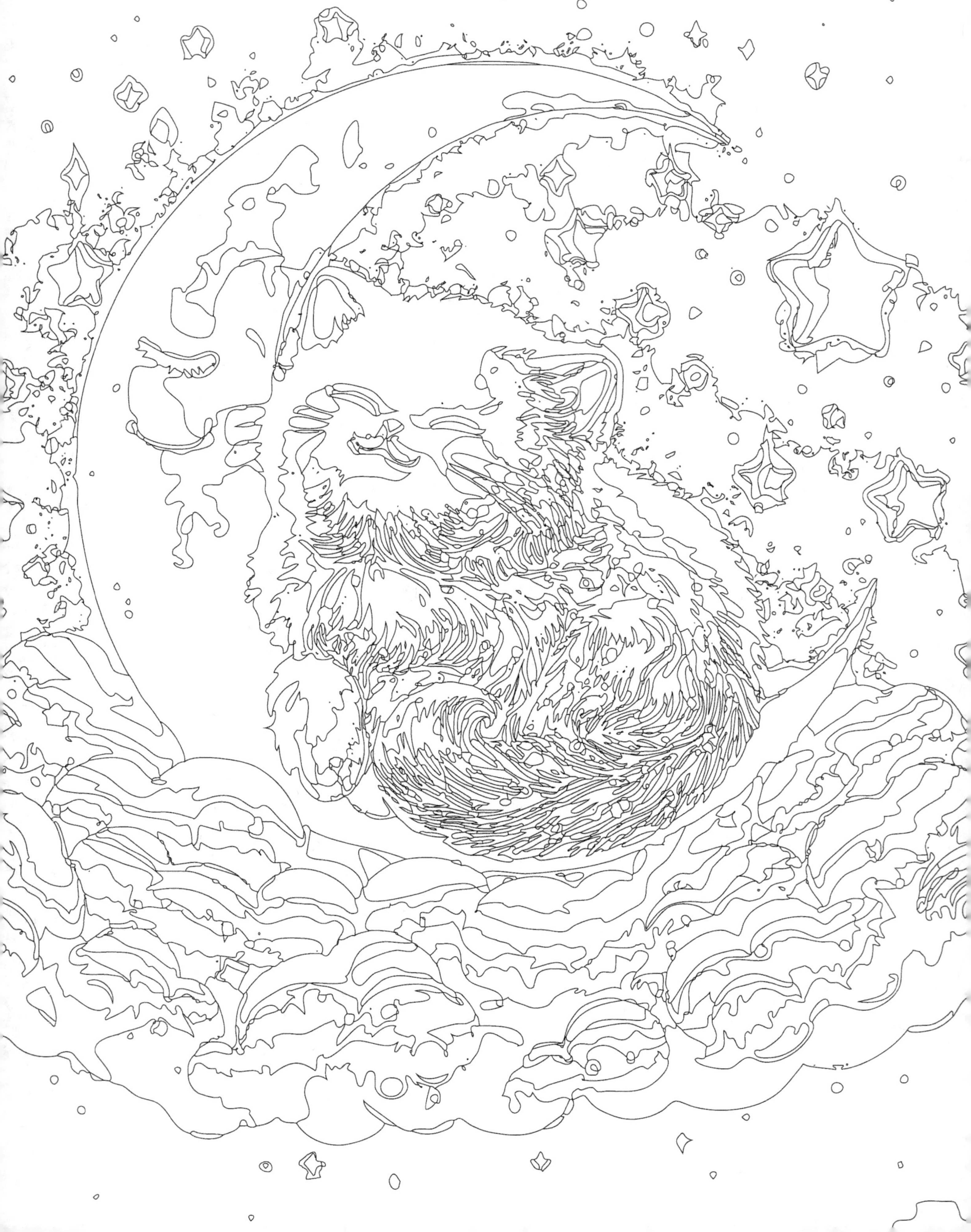

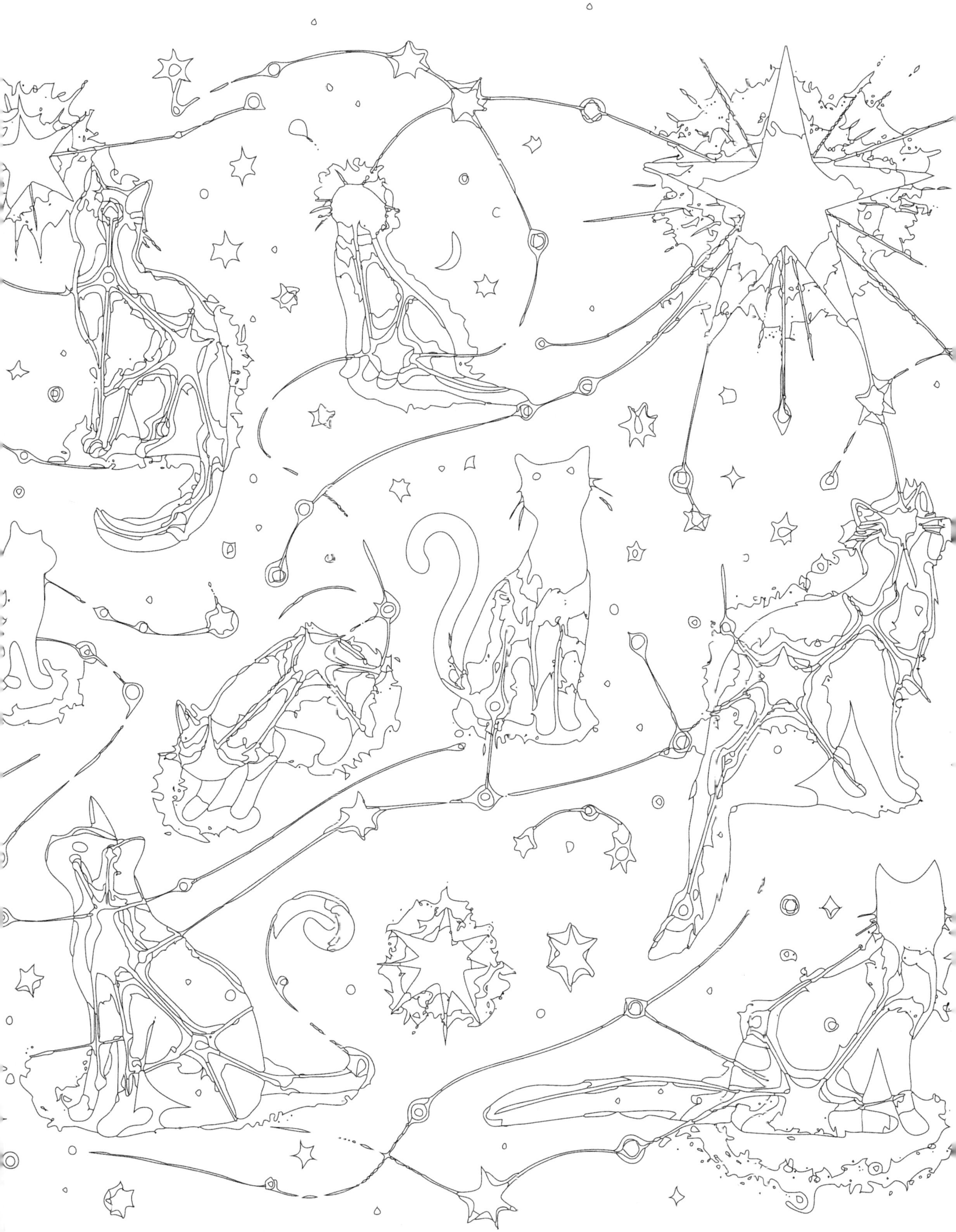

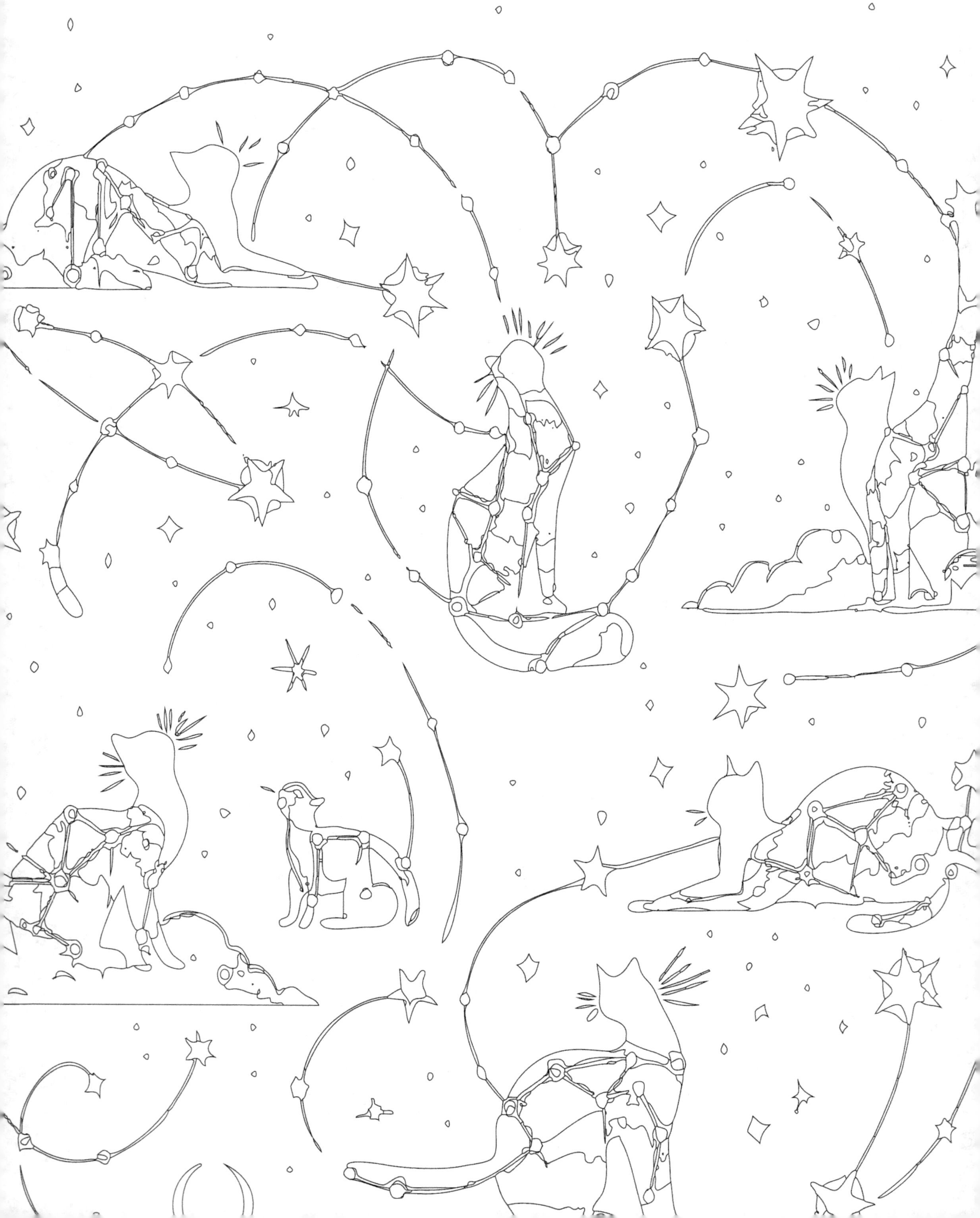

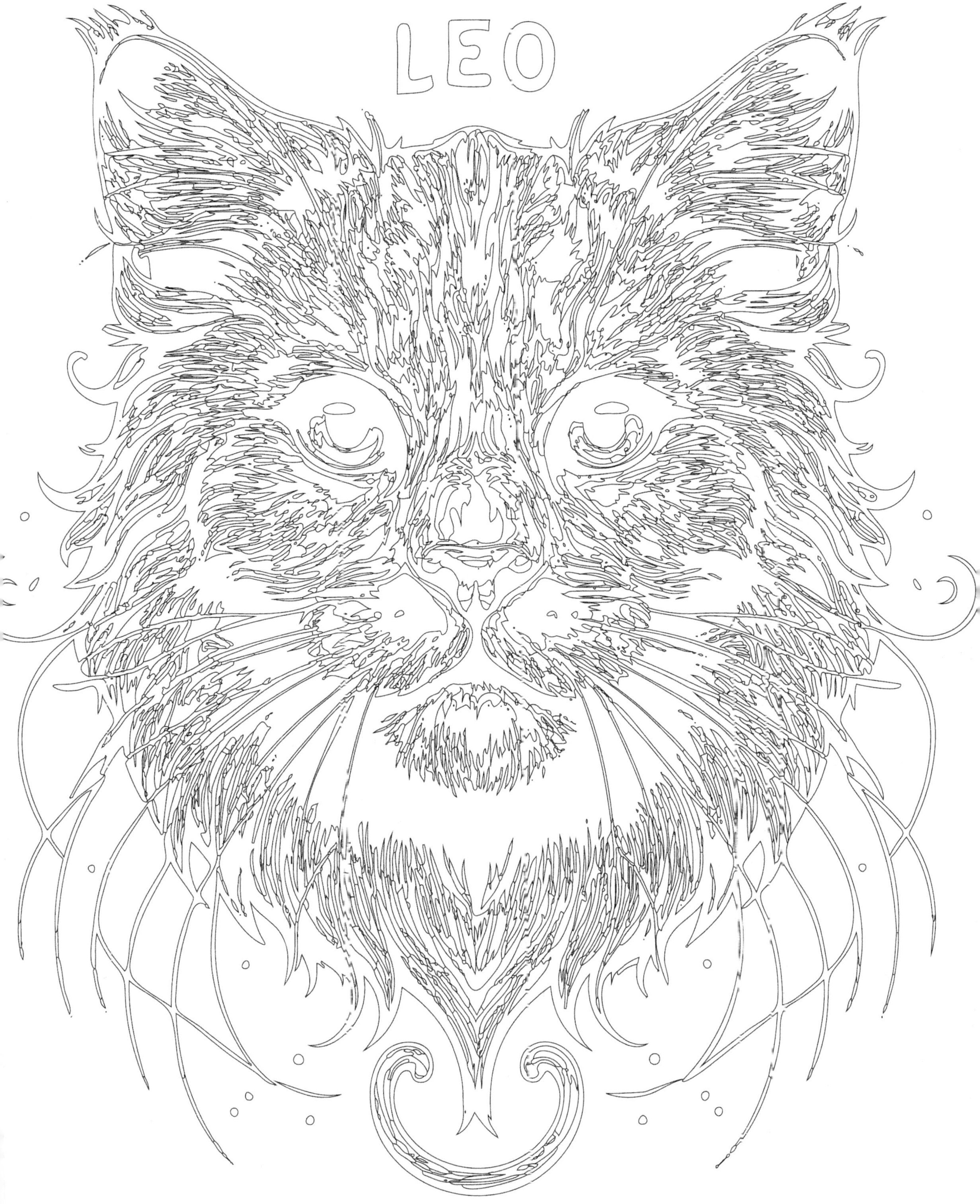
LEO

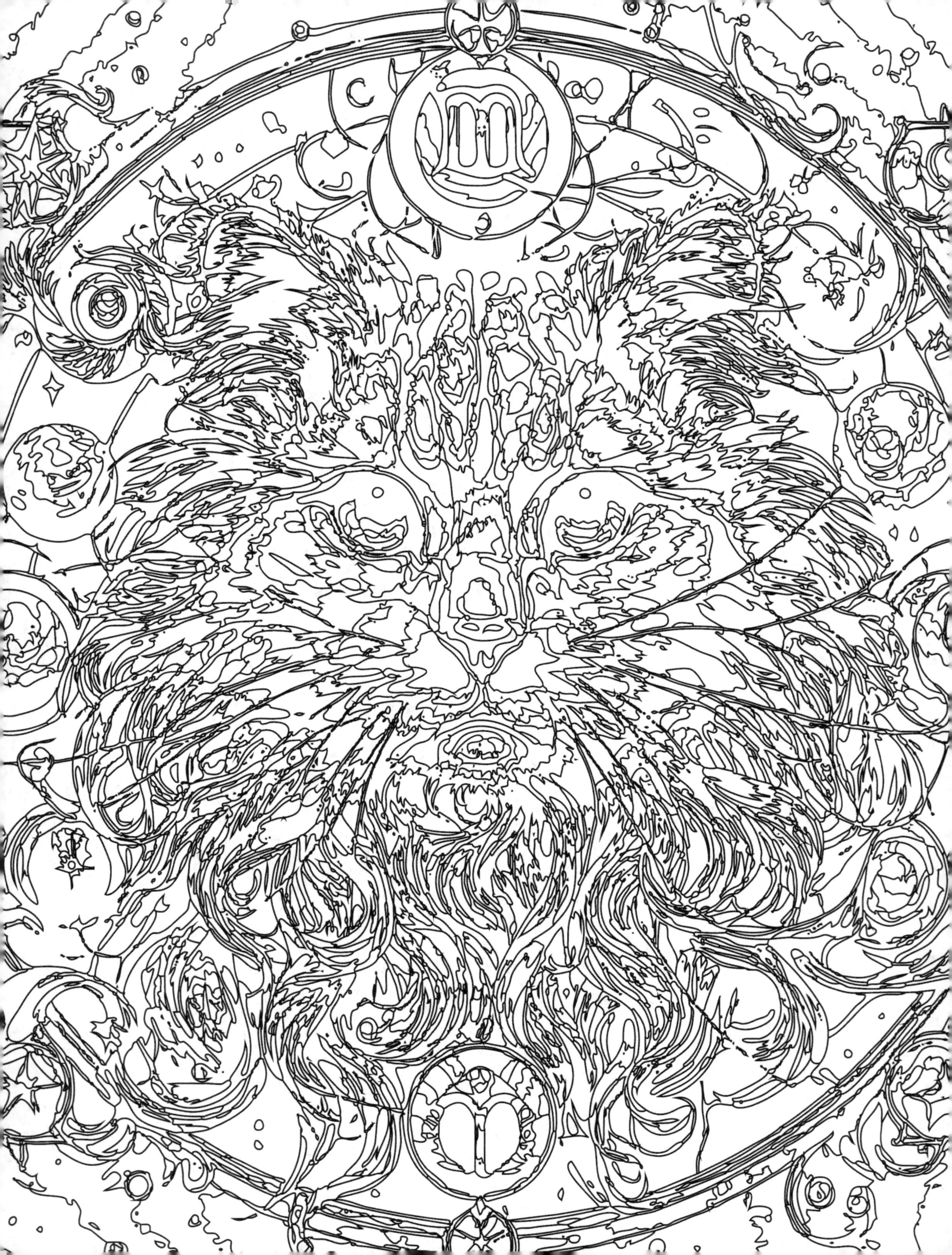

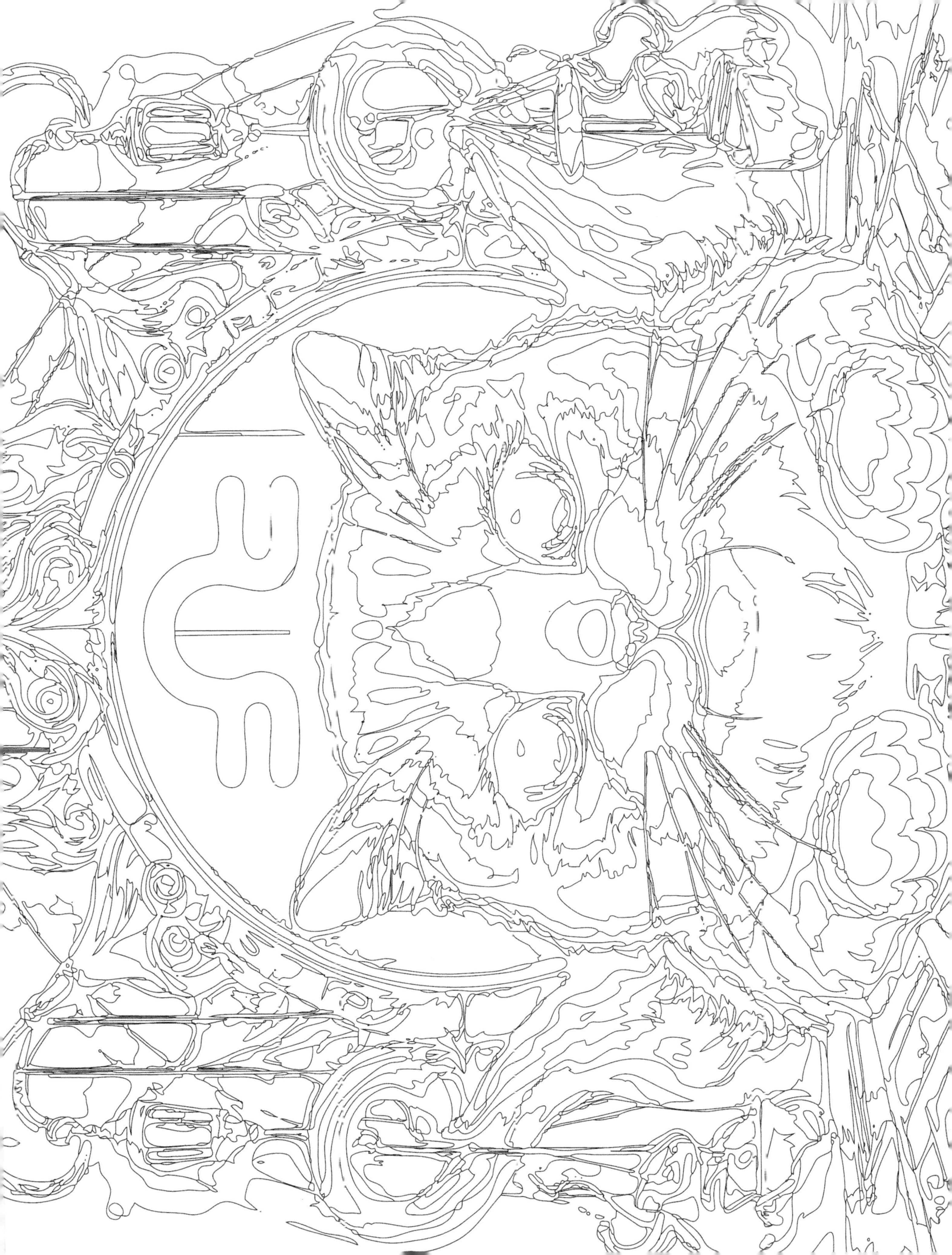

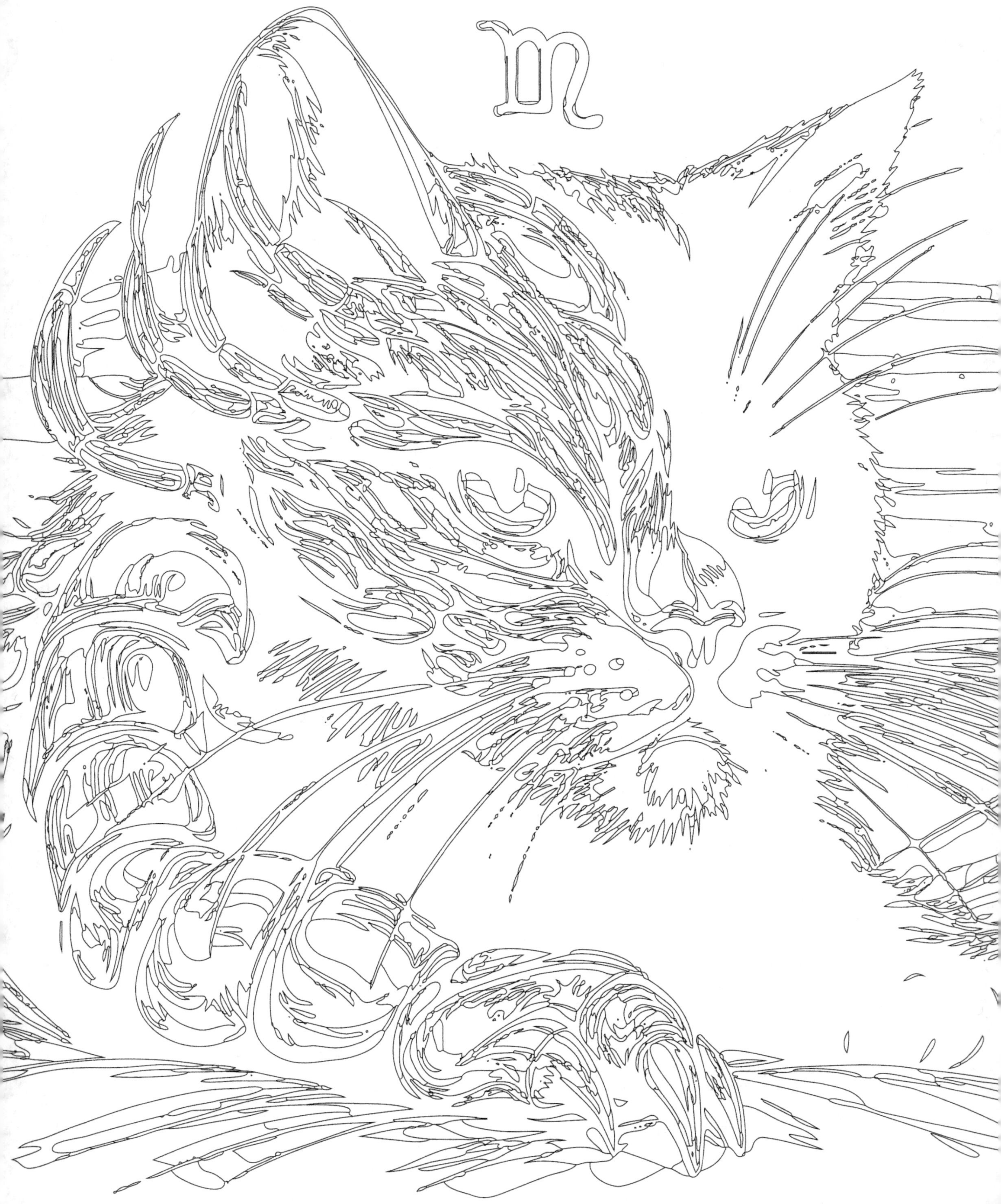

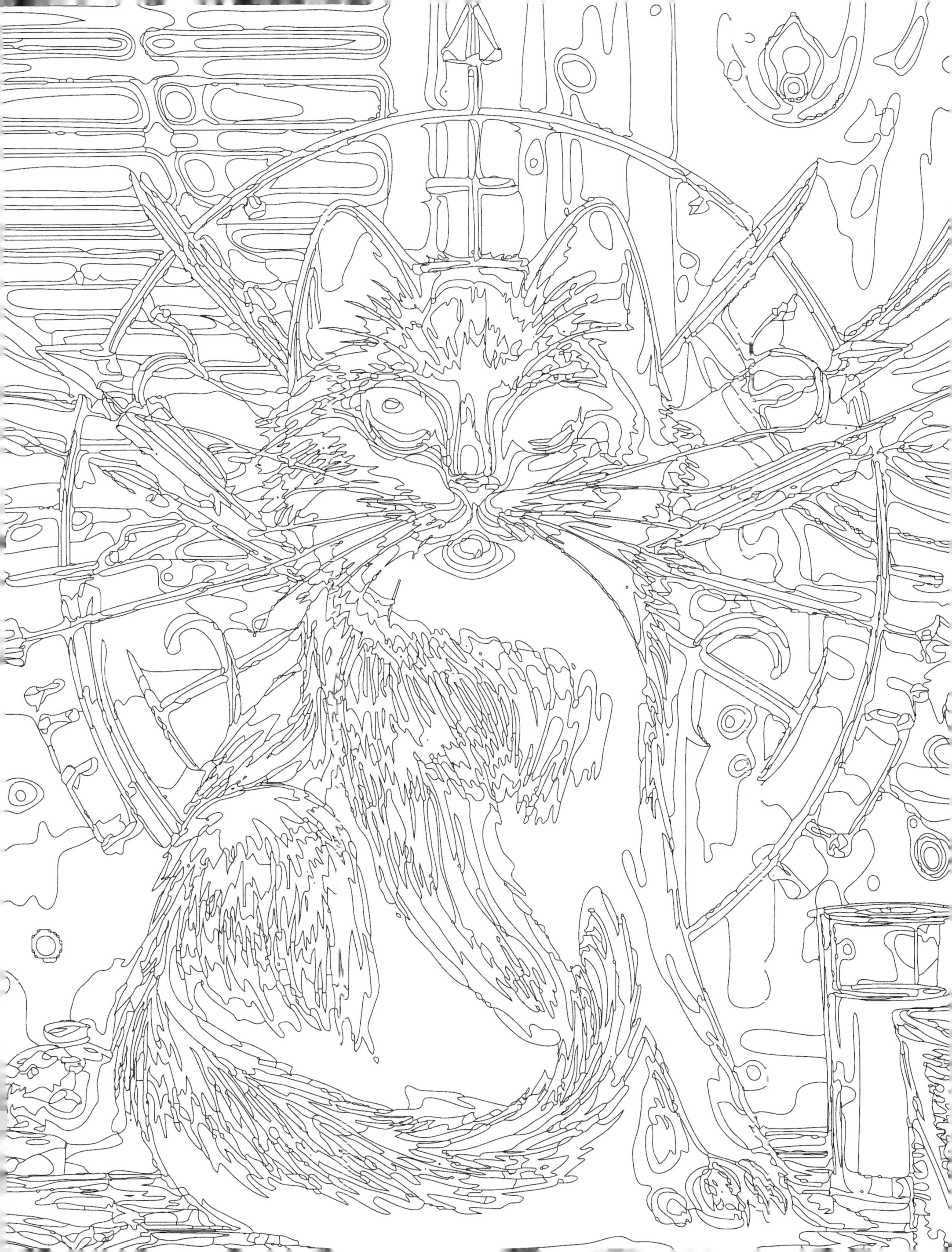

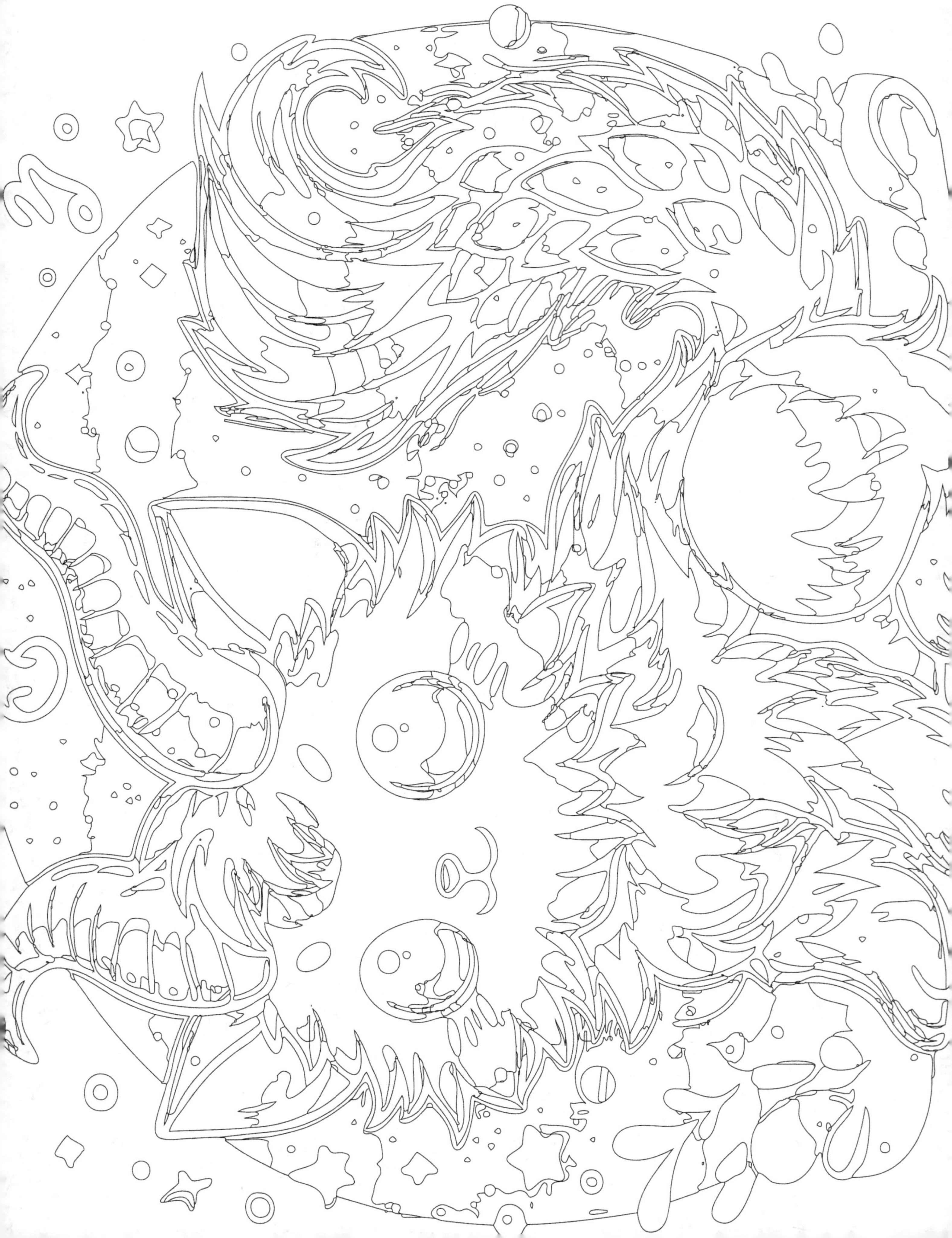

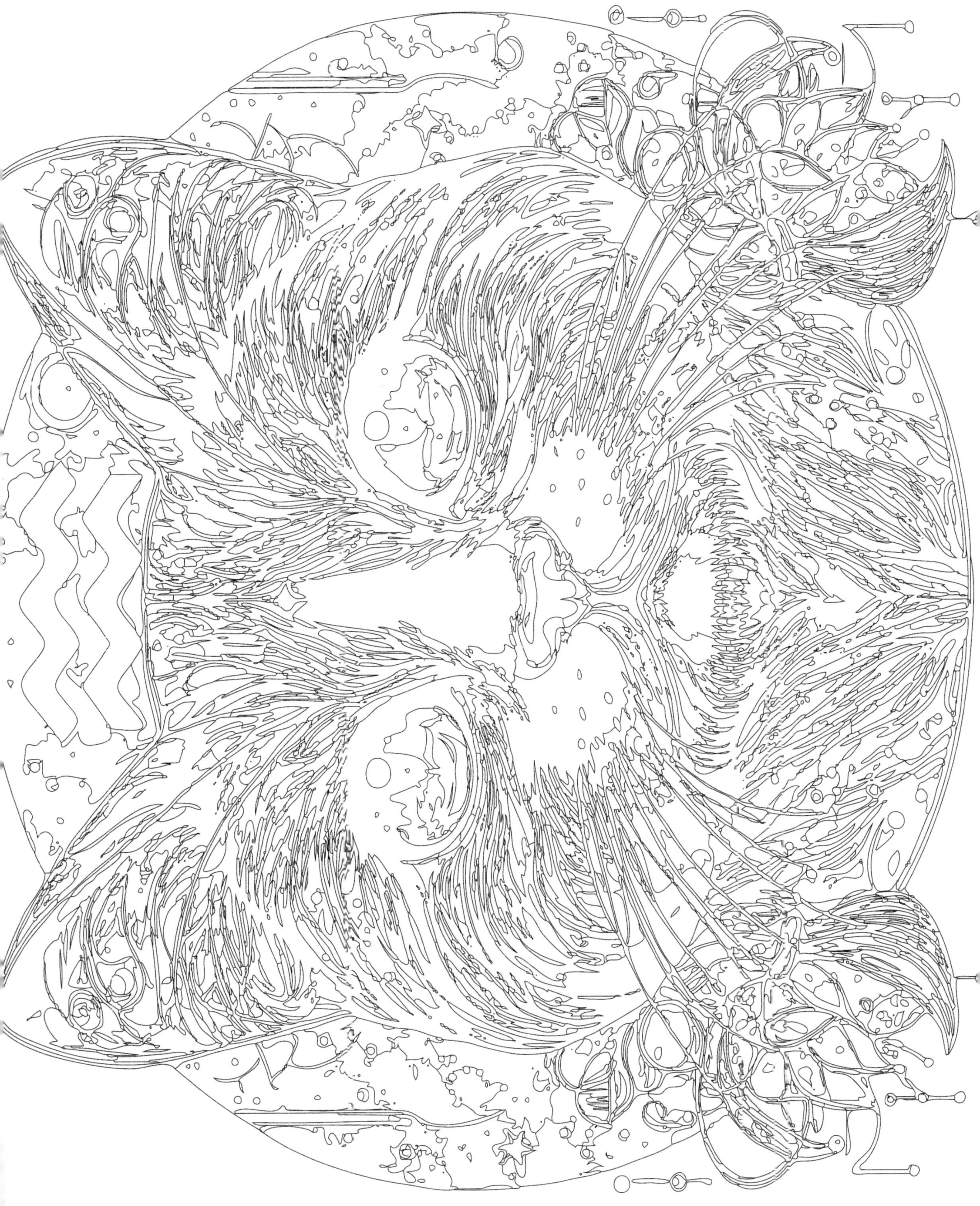

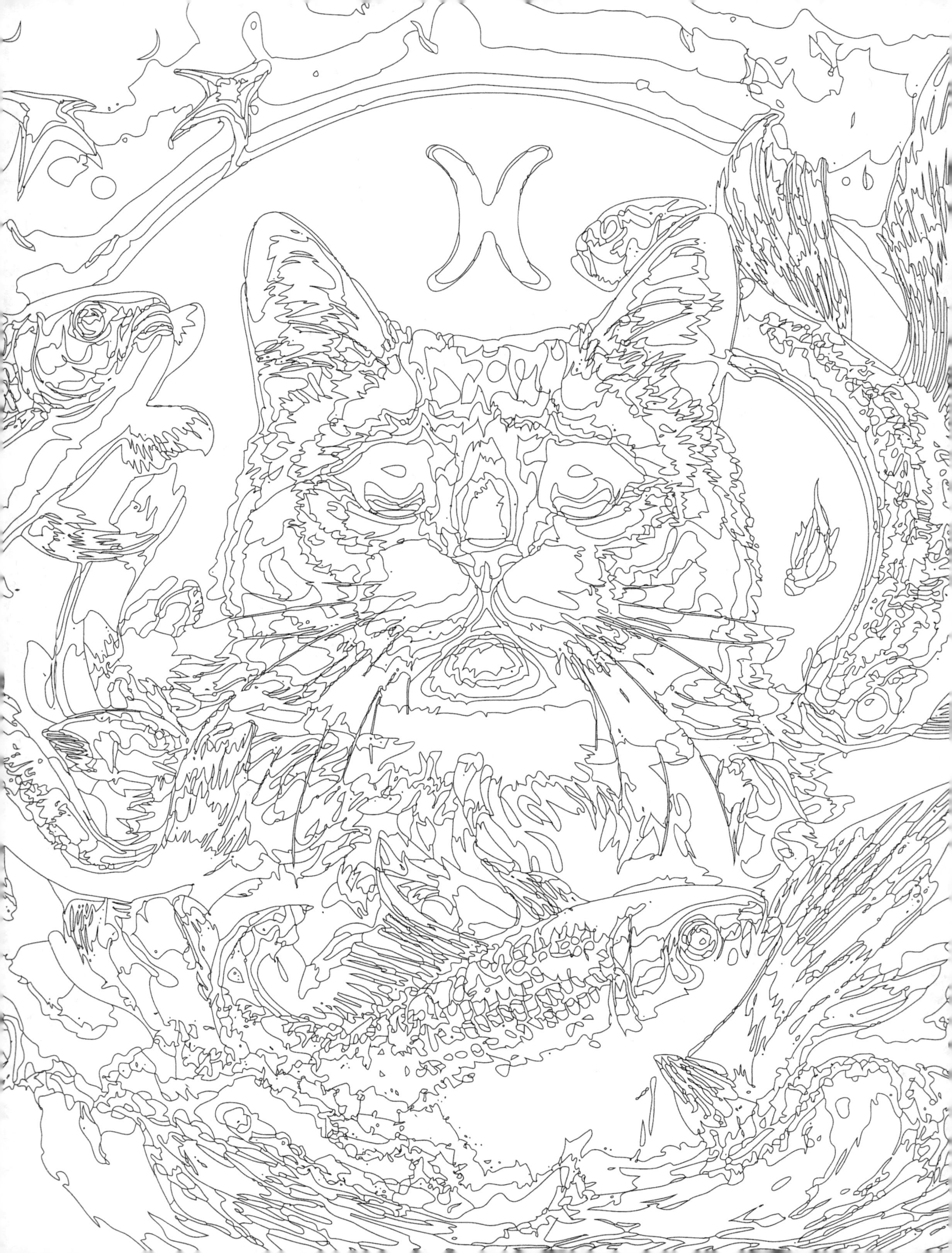

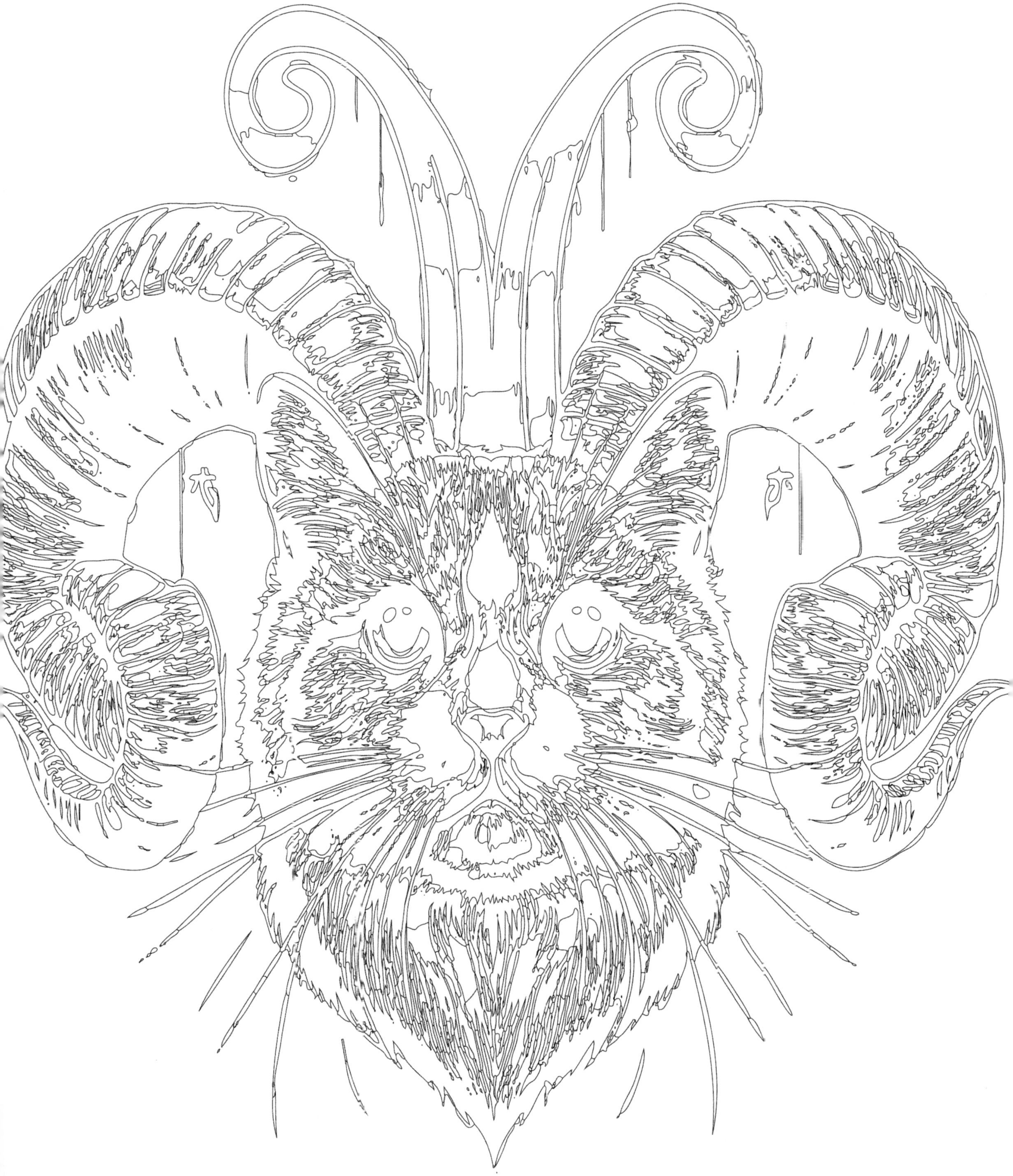

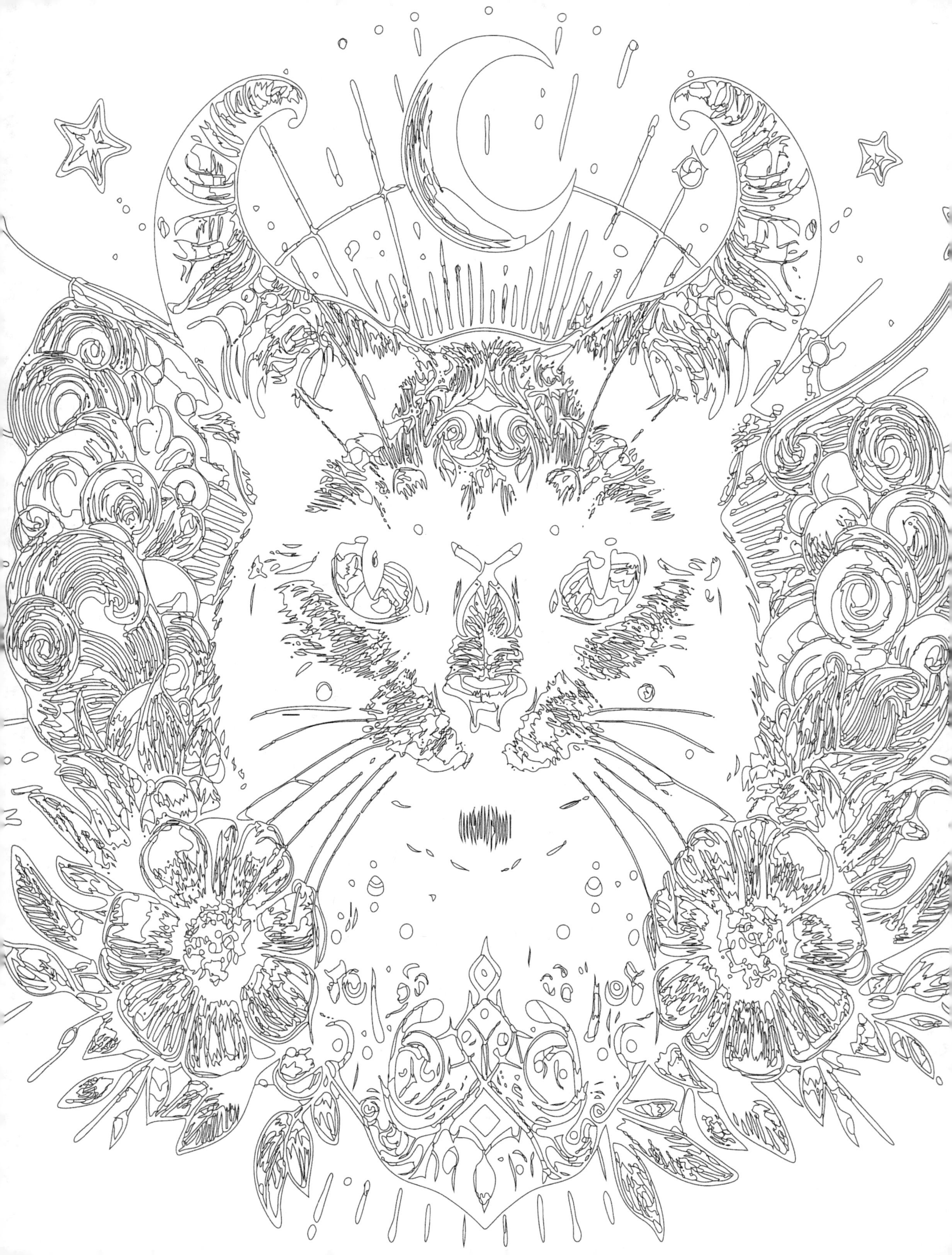

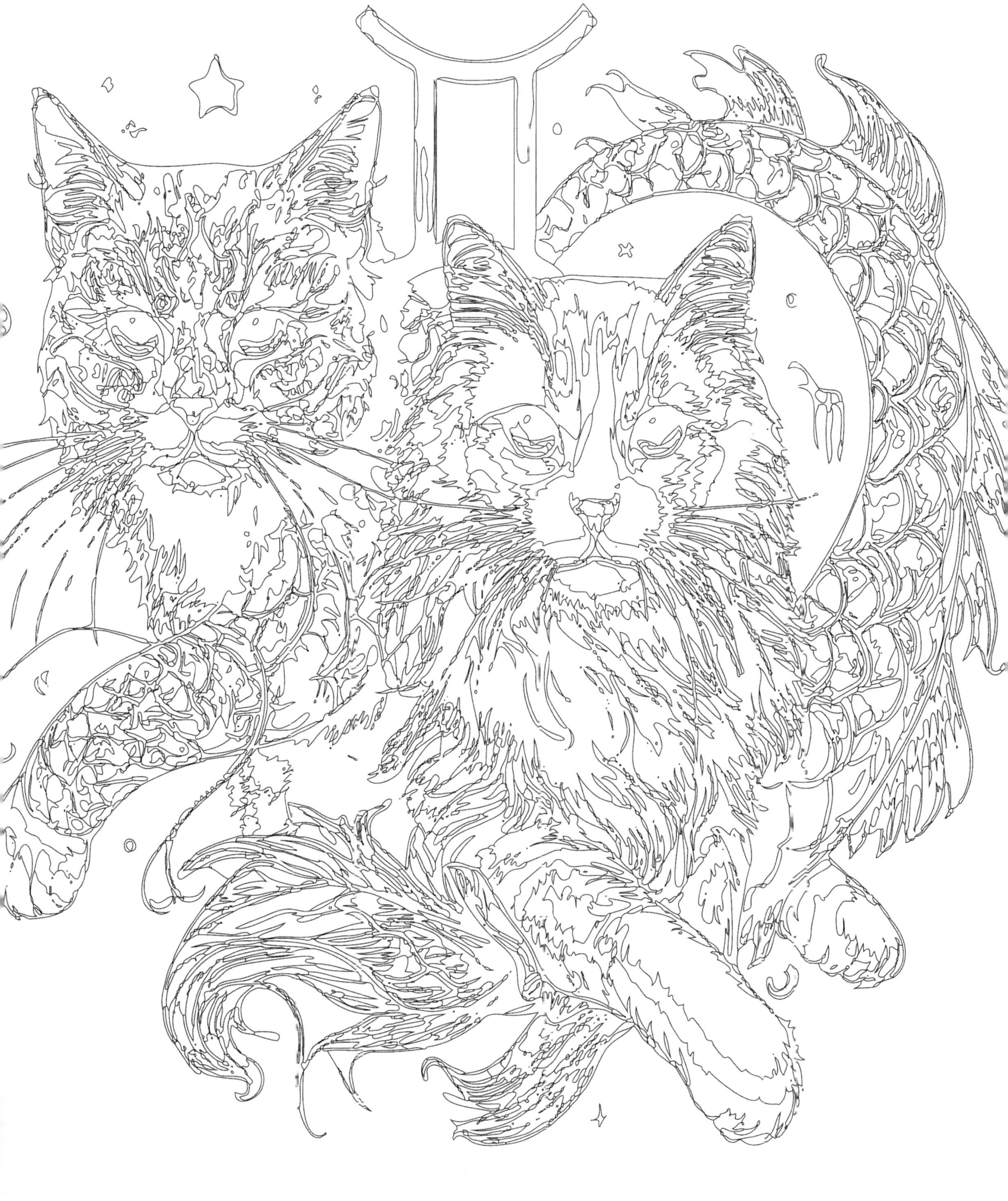

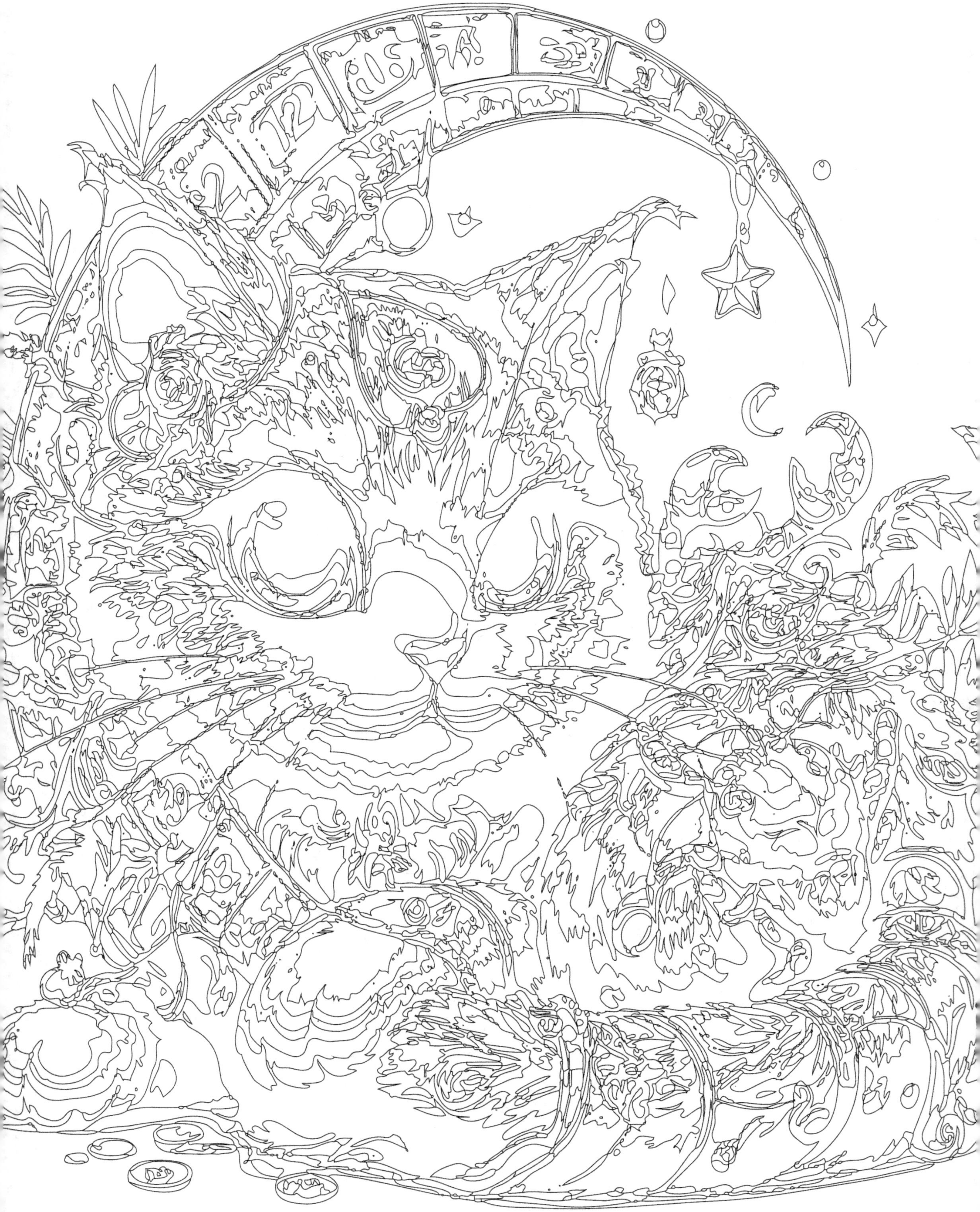

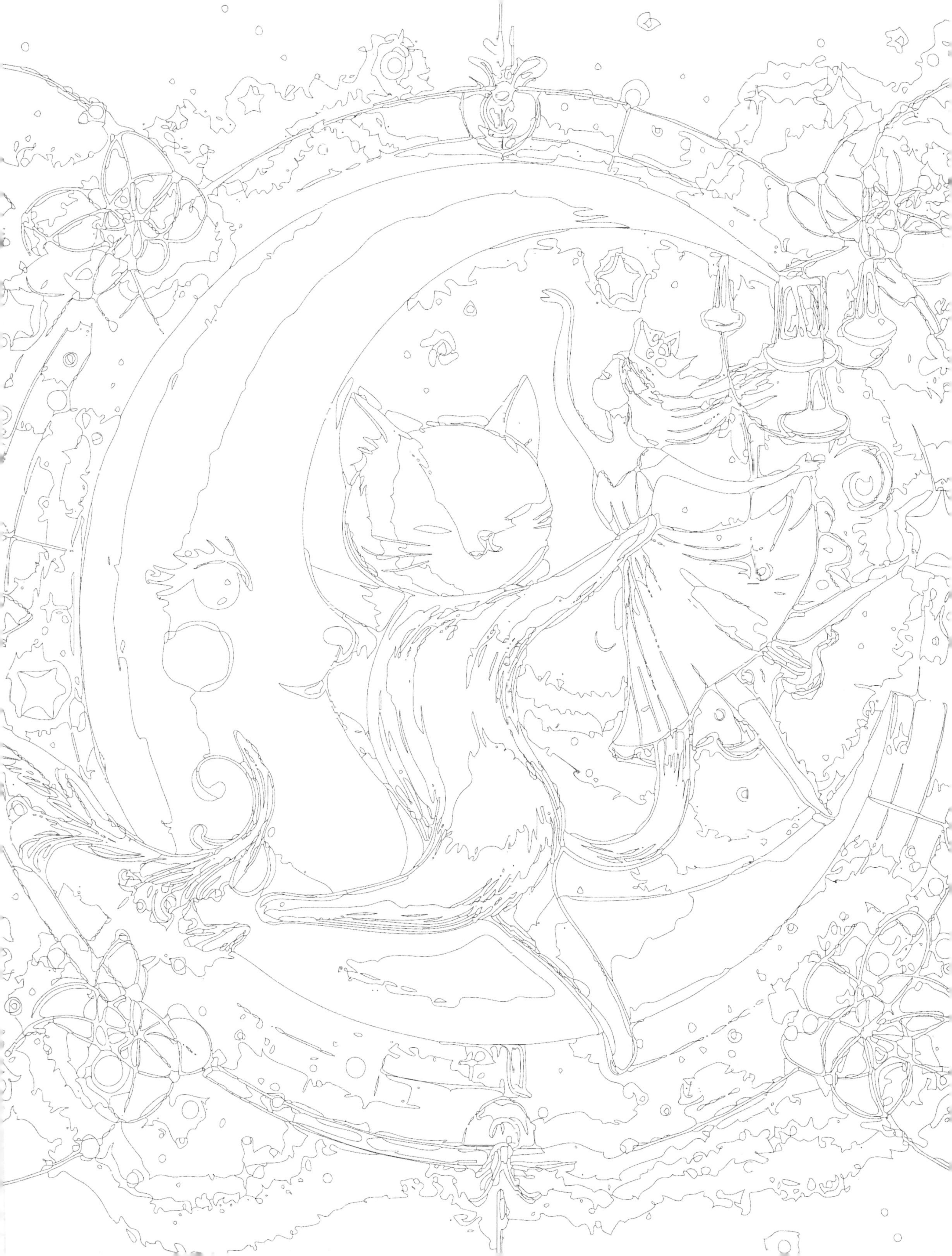

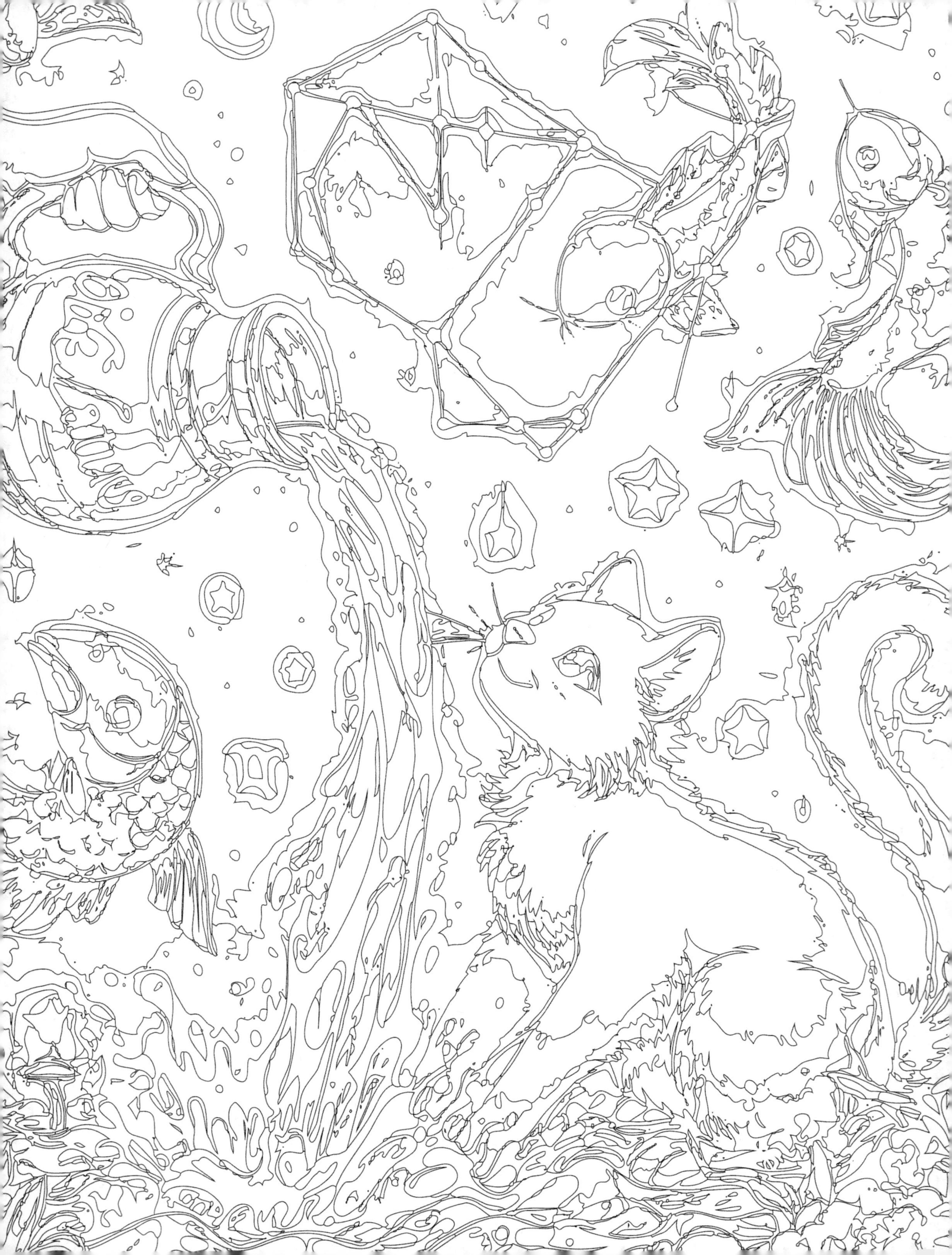

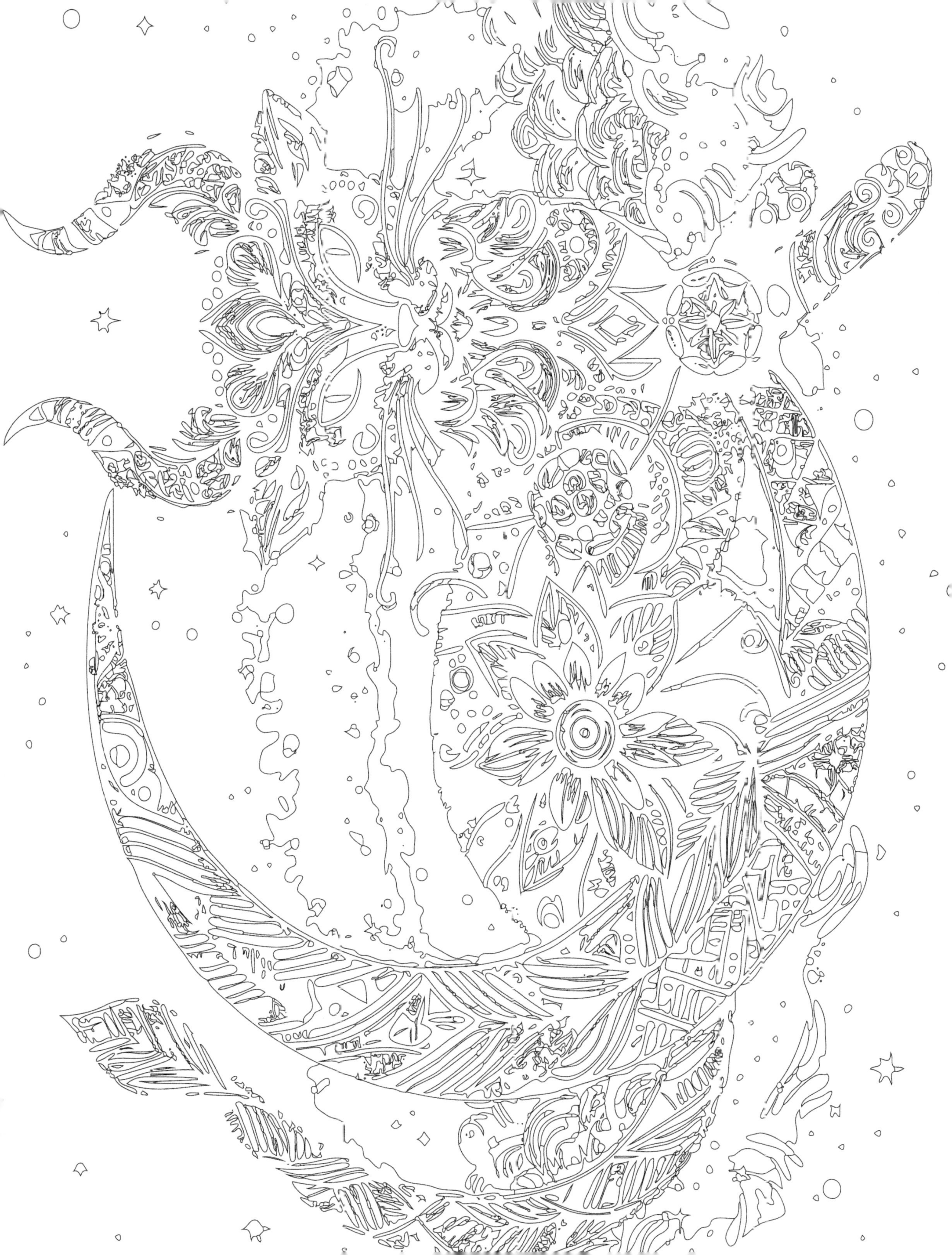

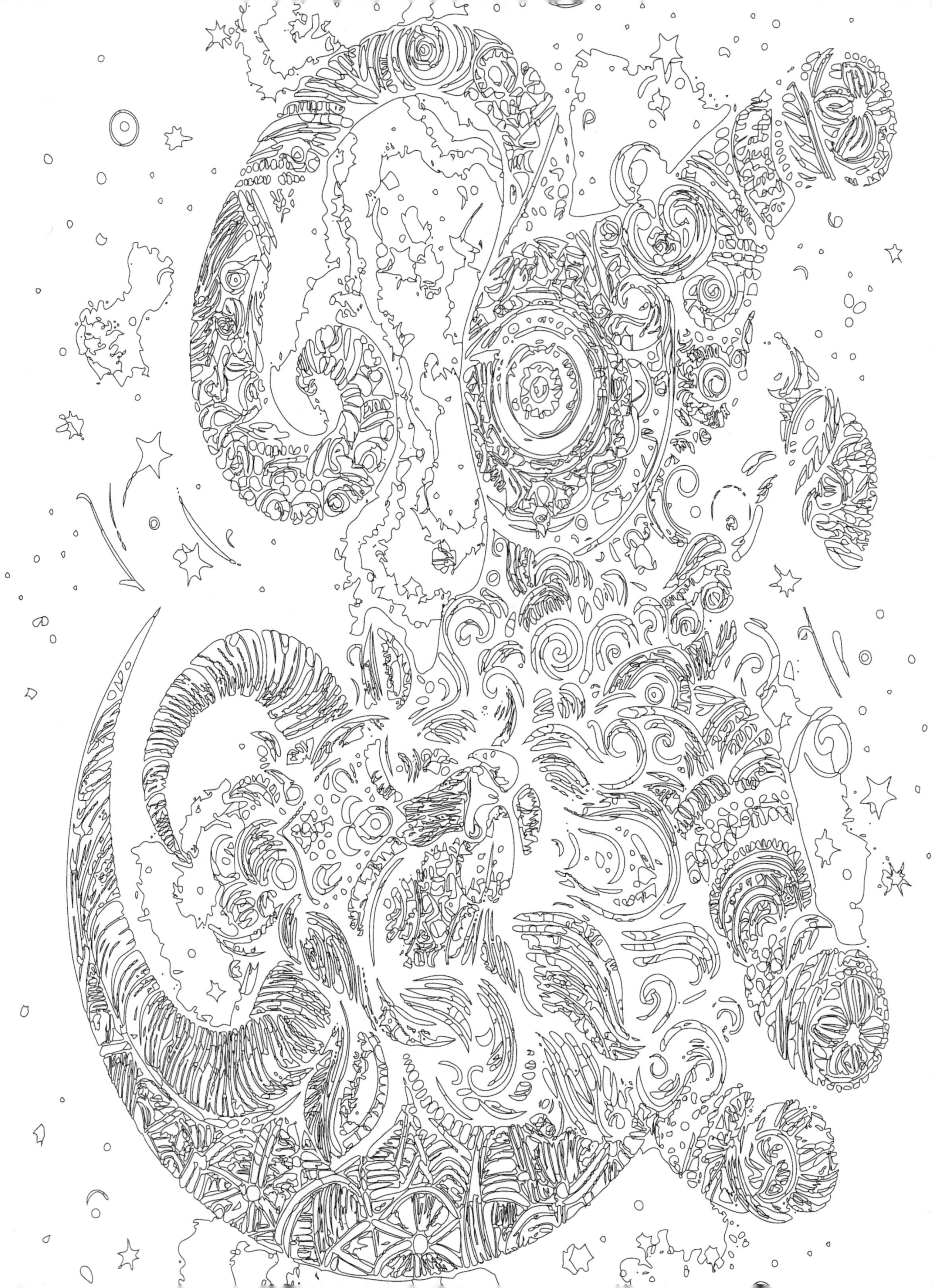

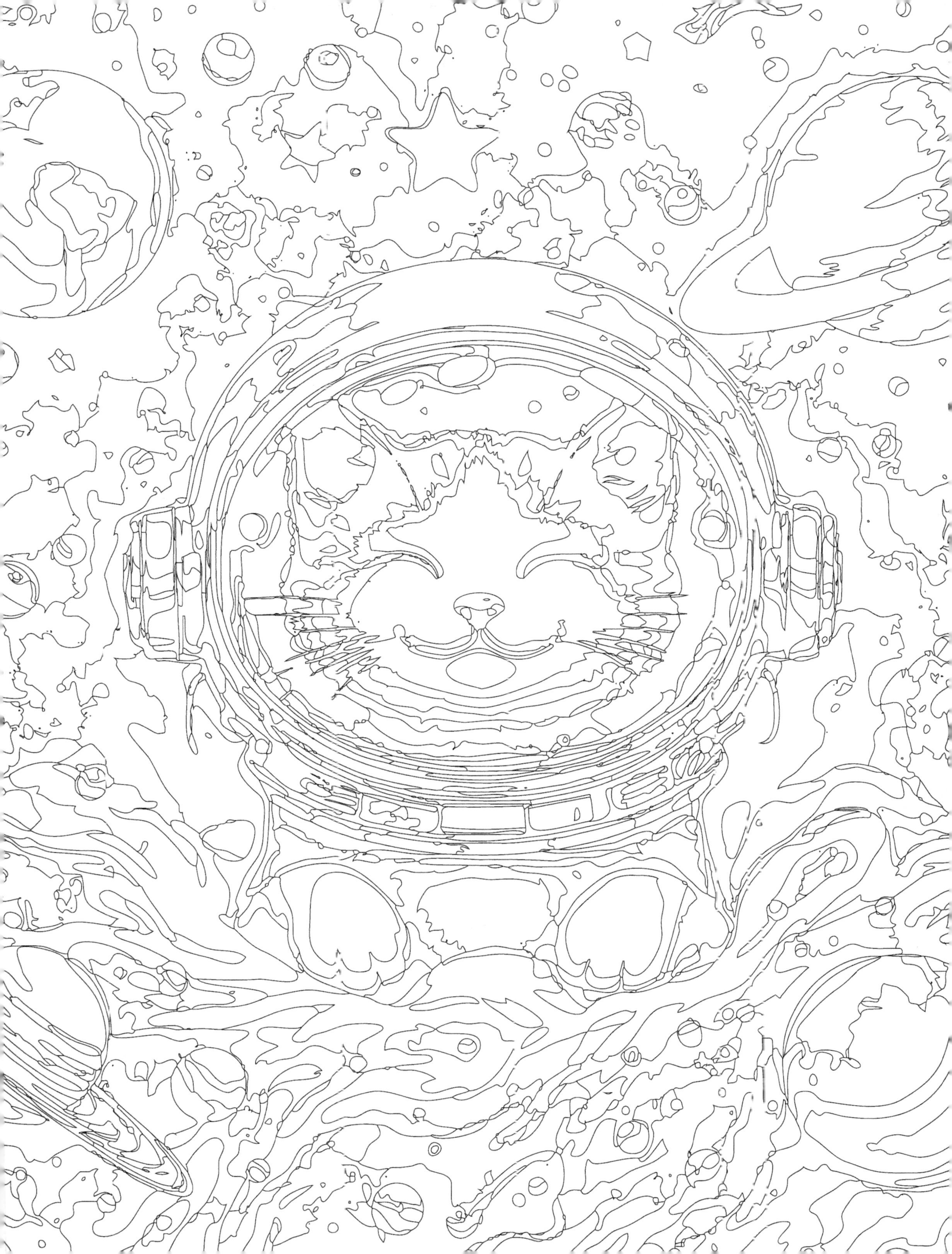

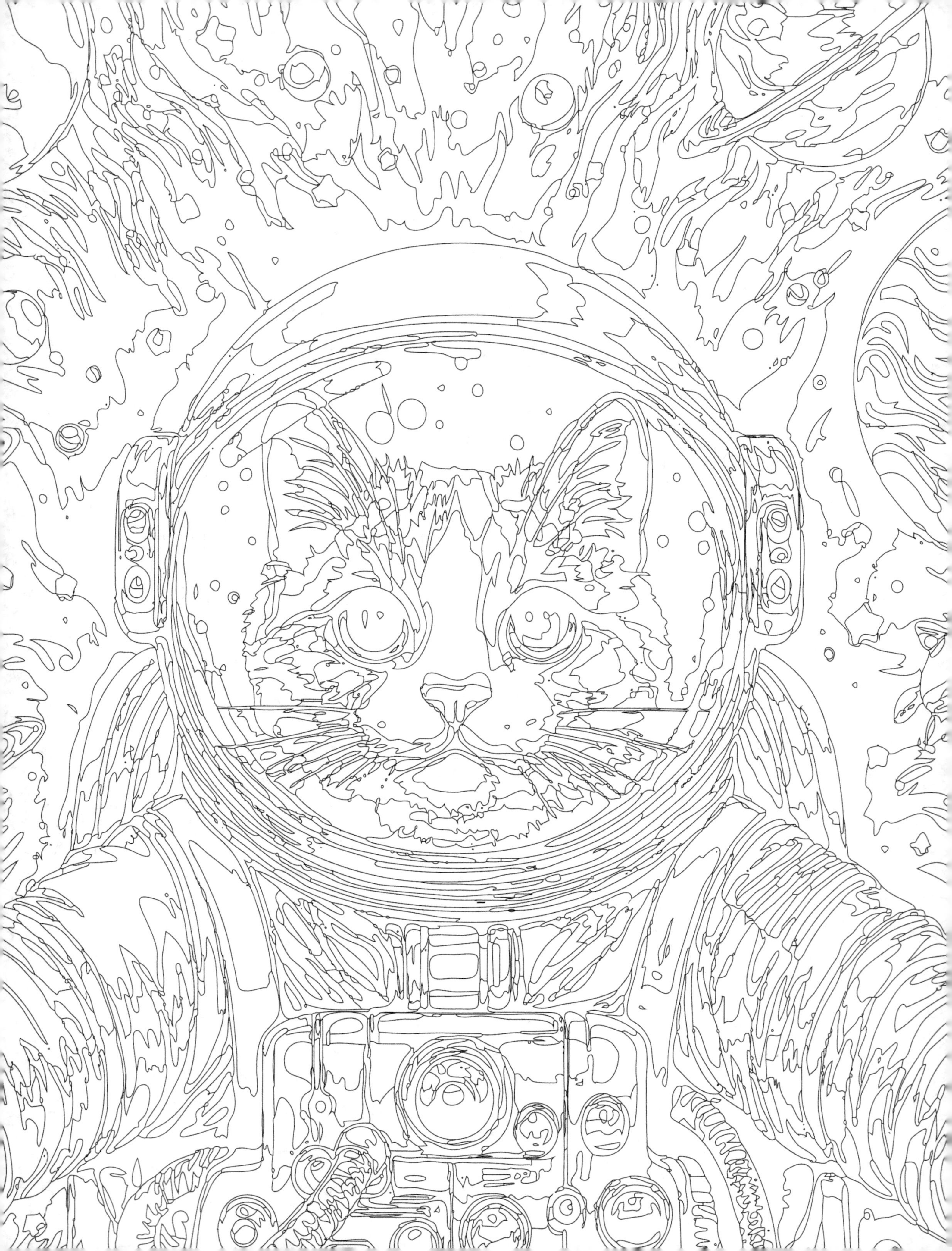

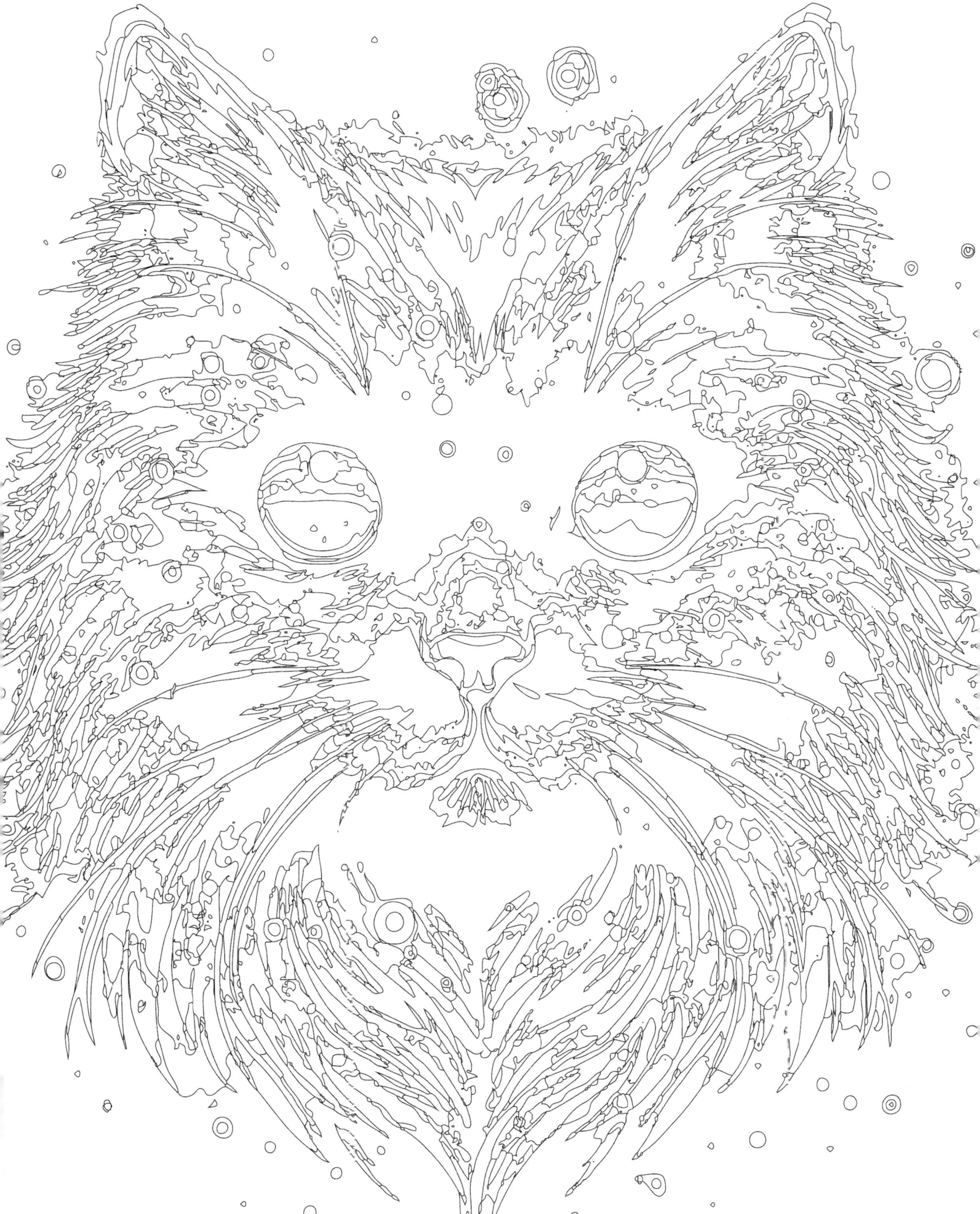

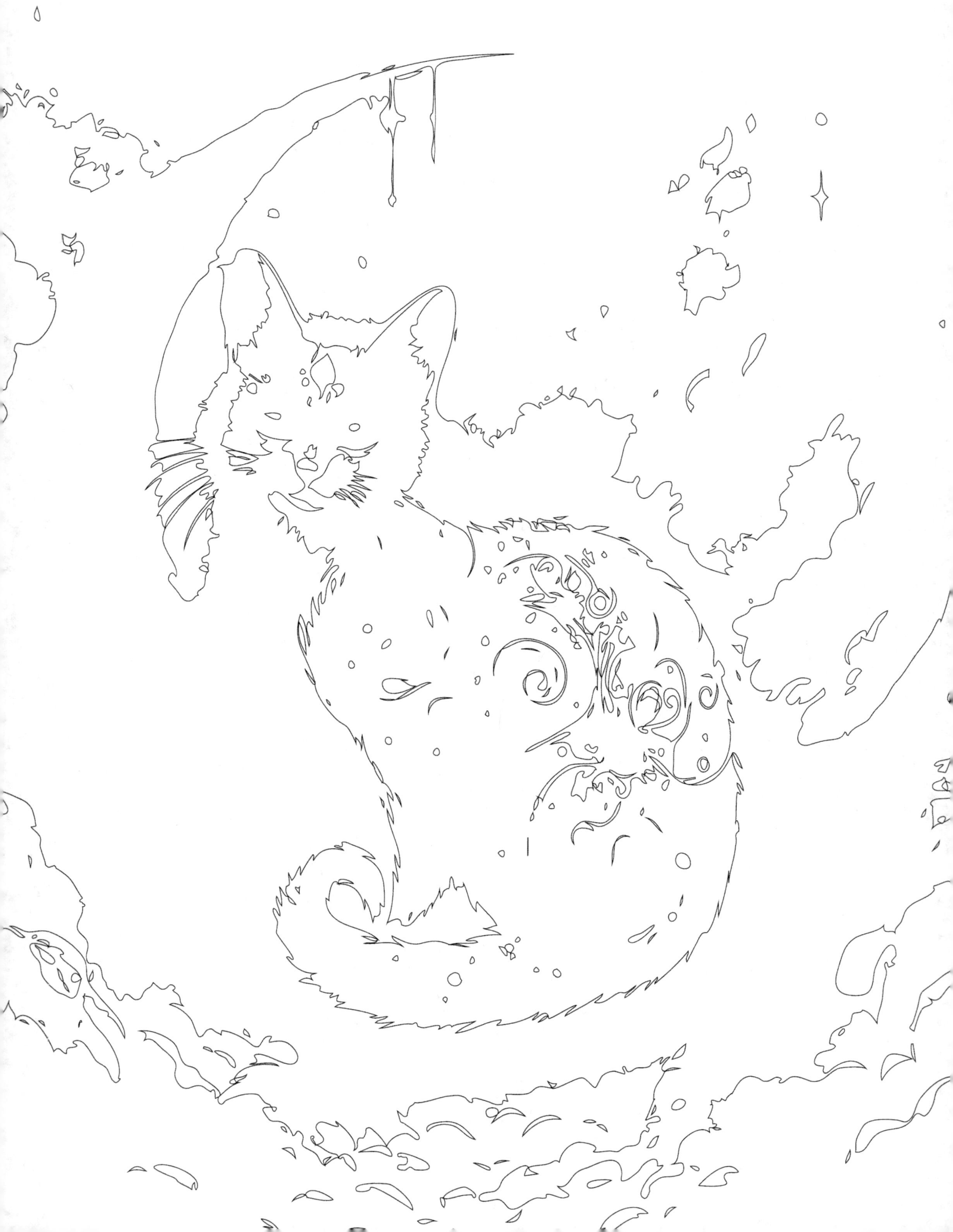

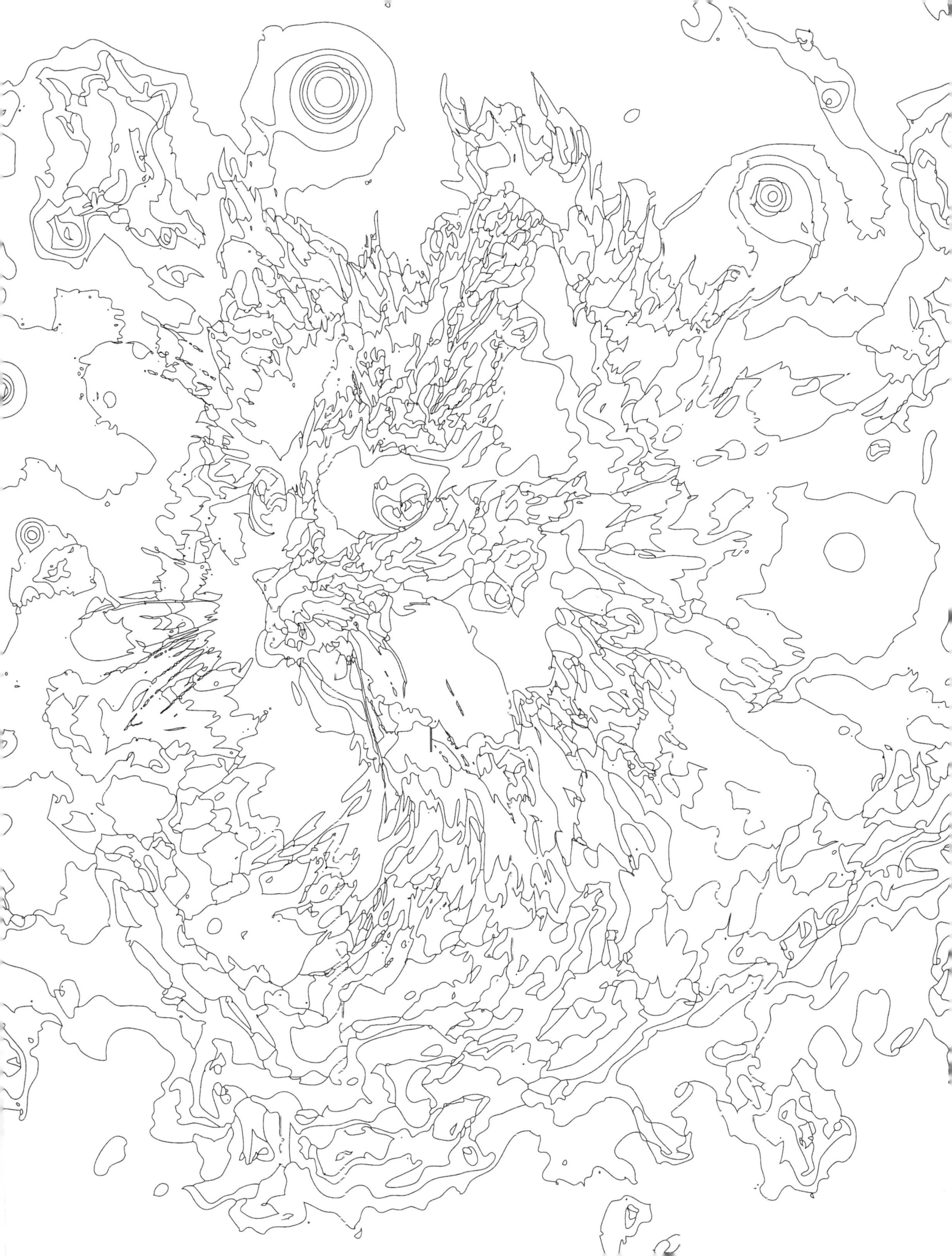

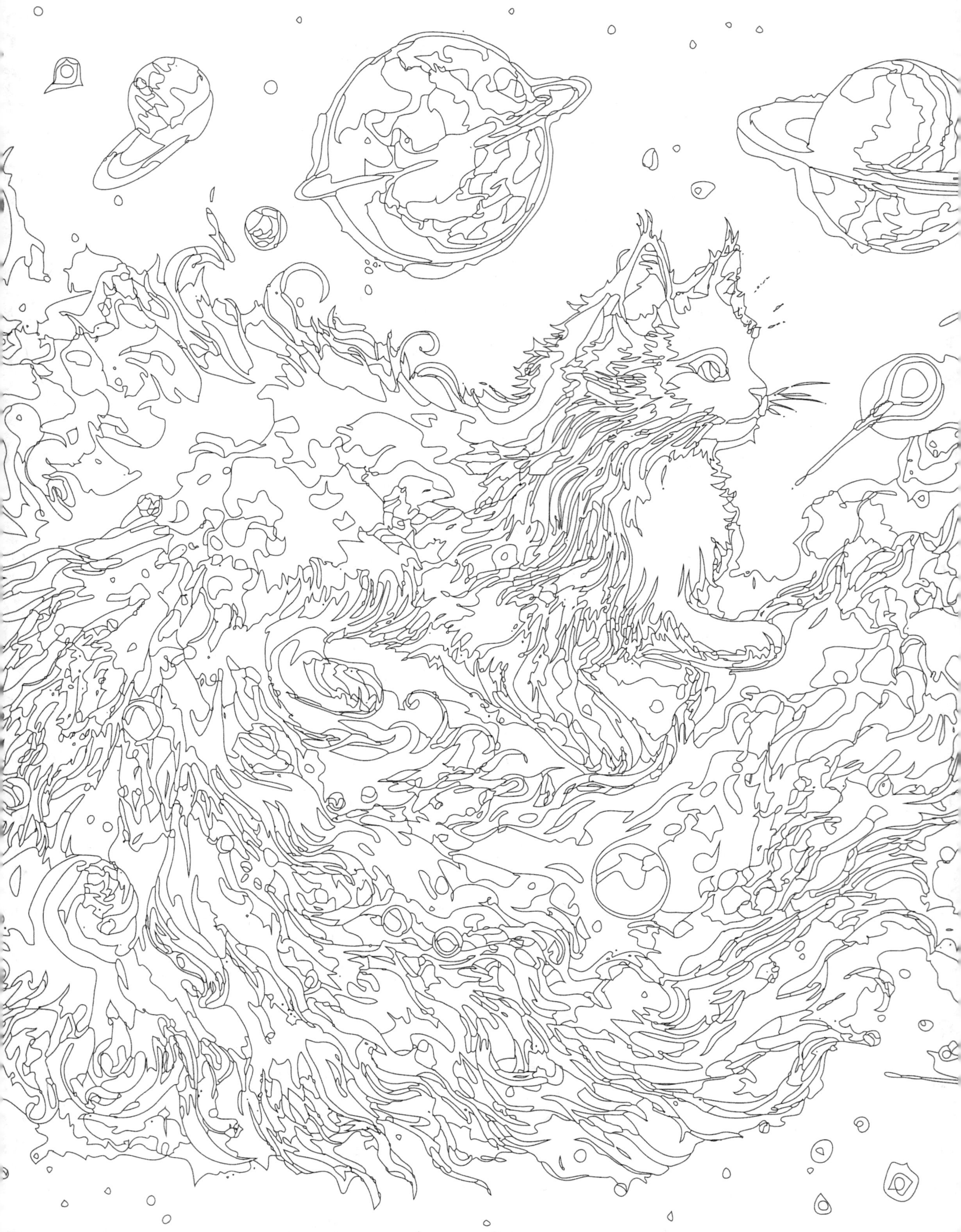

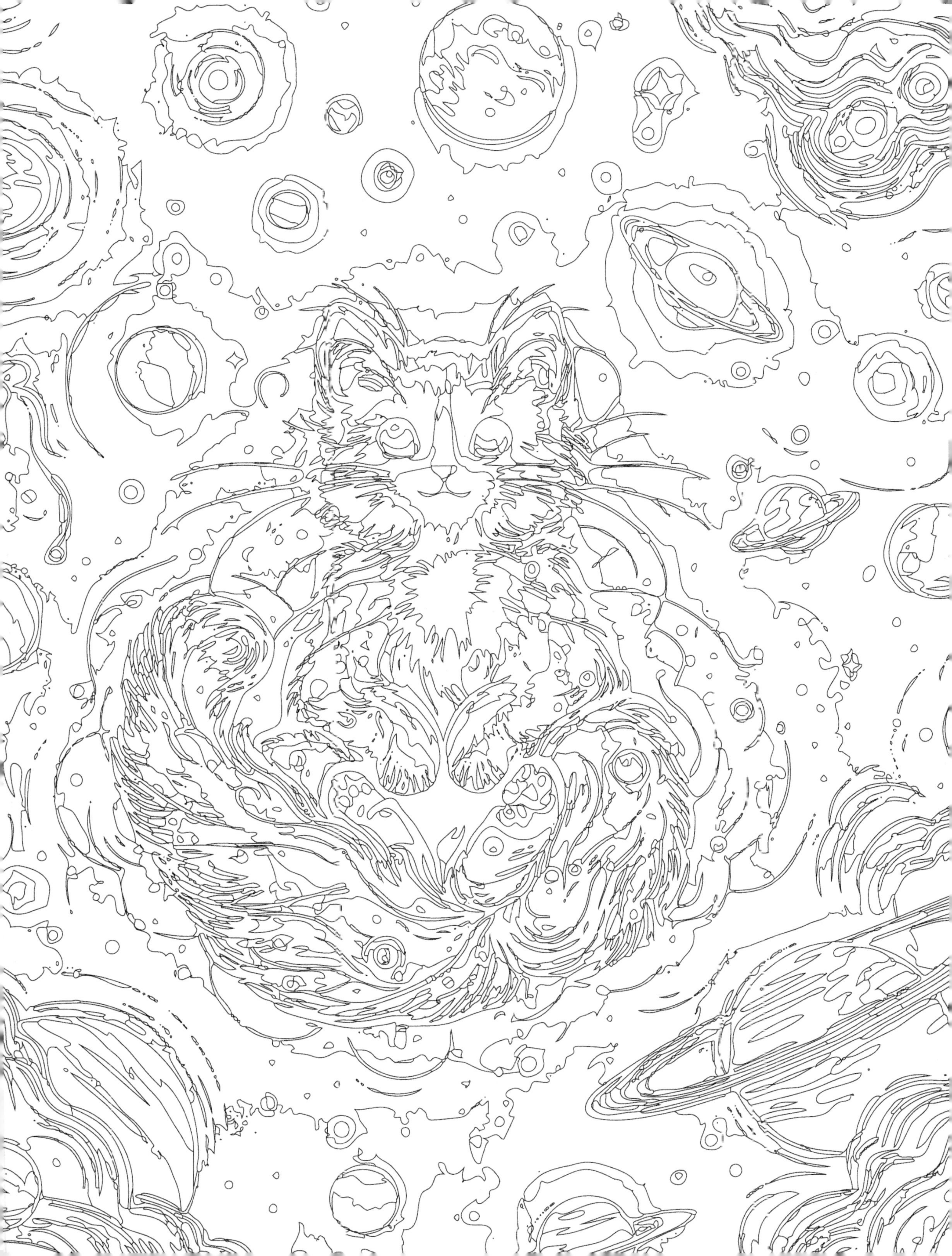

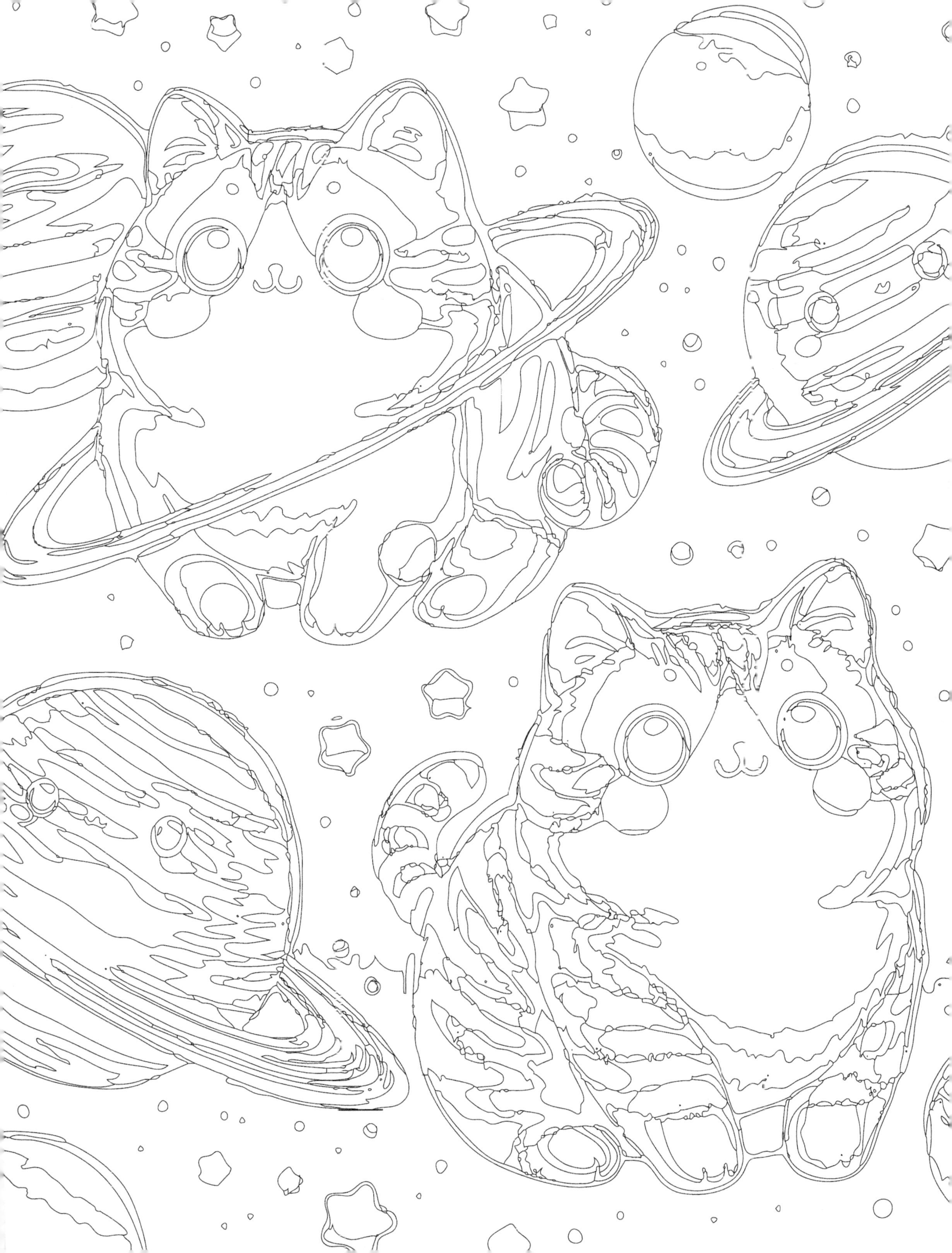

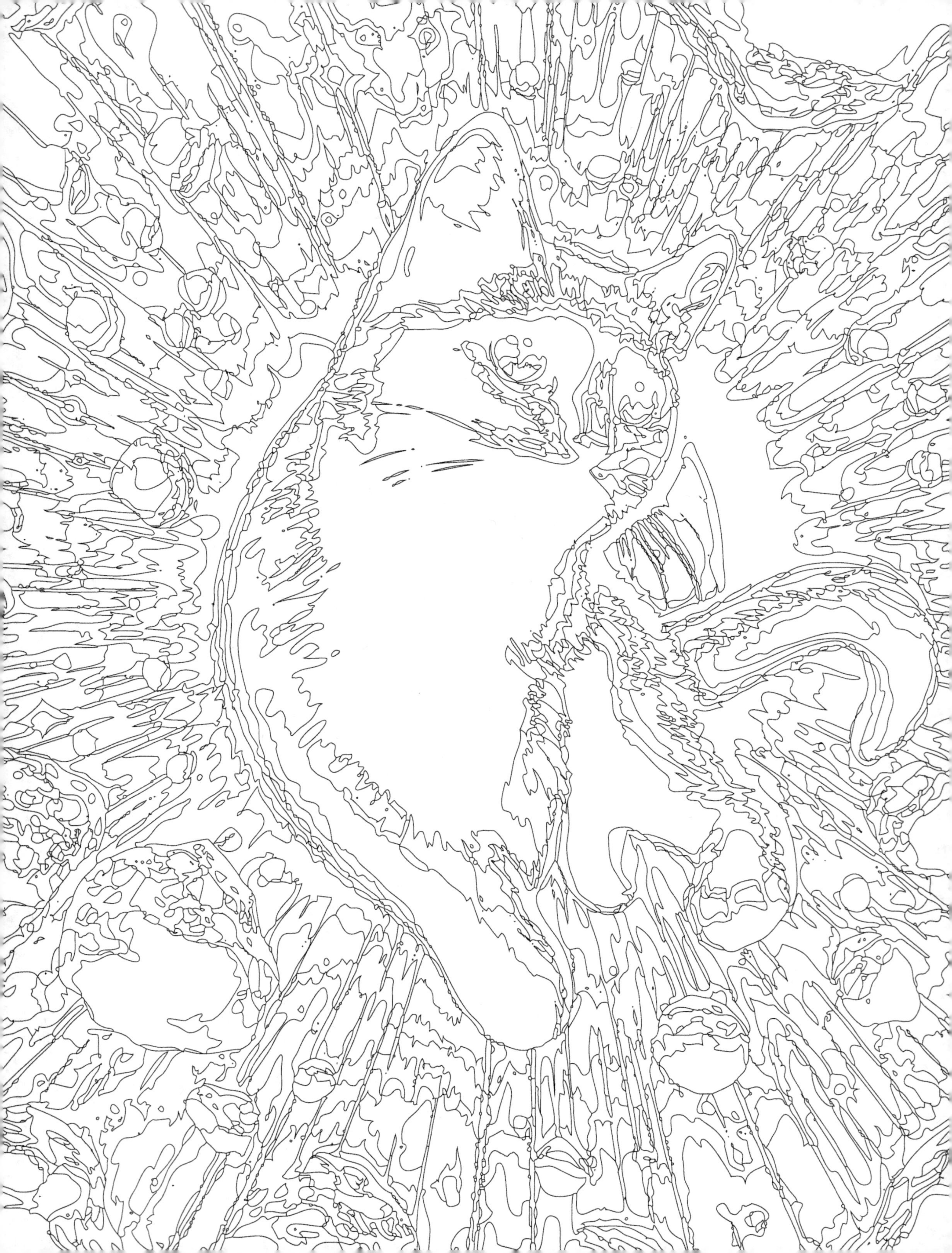

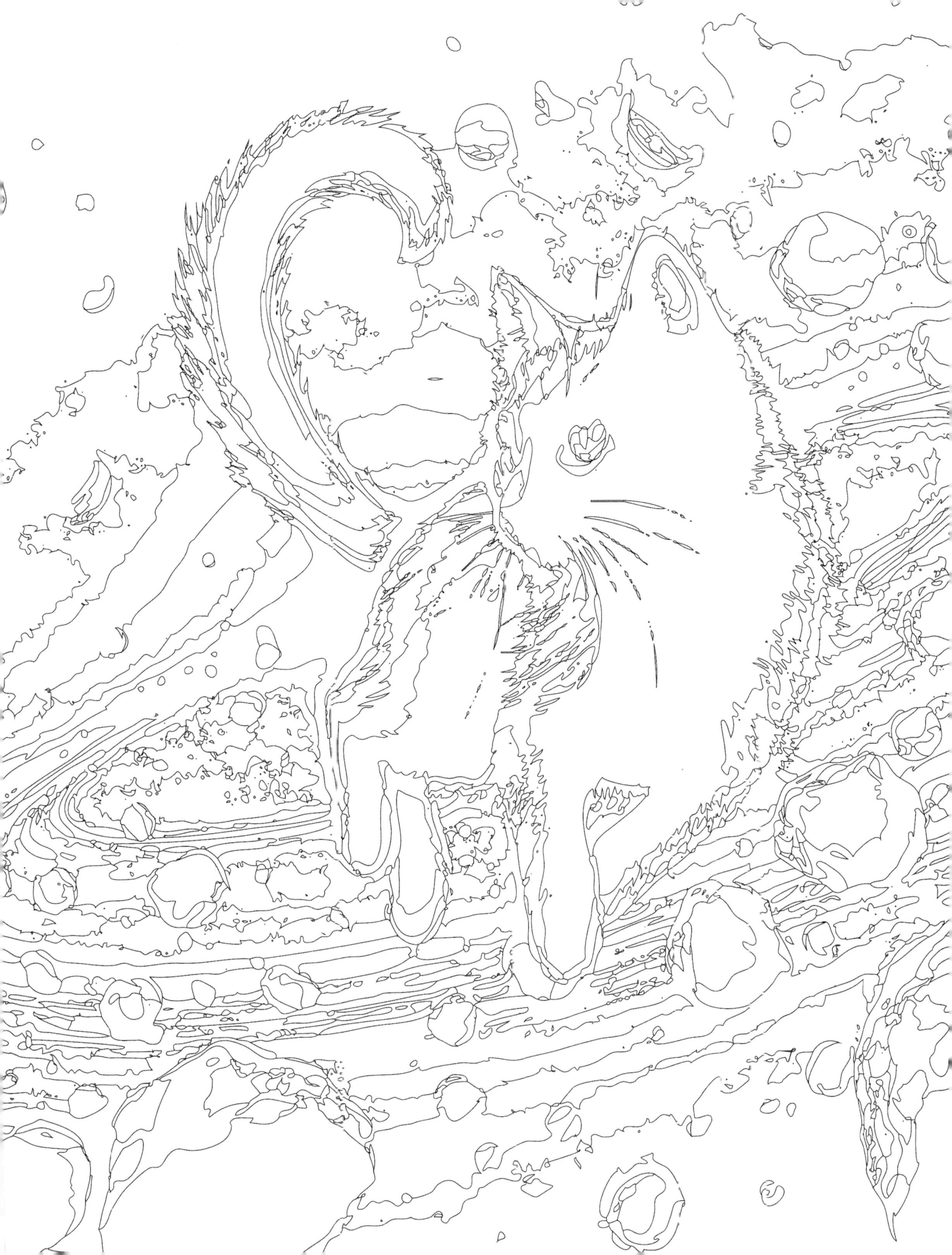

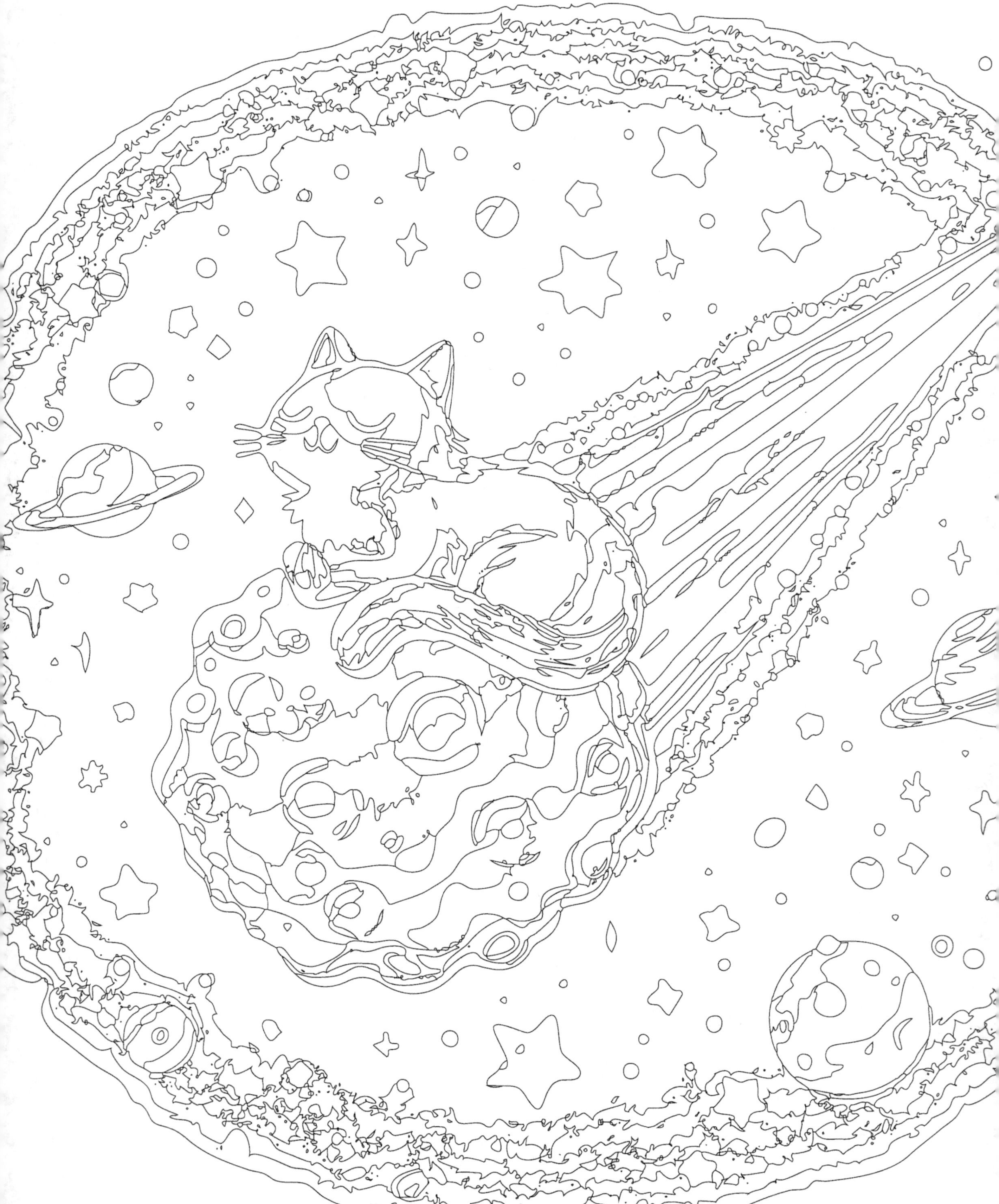

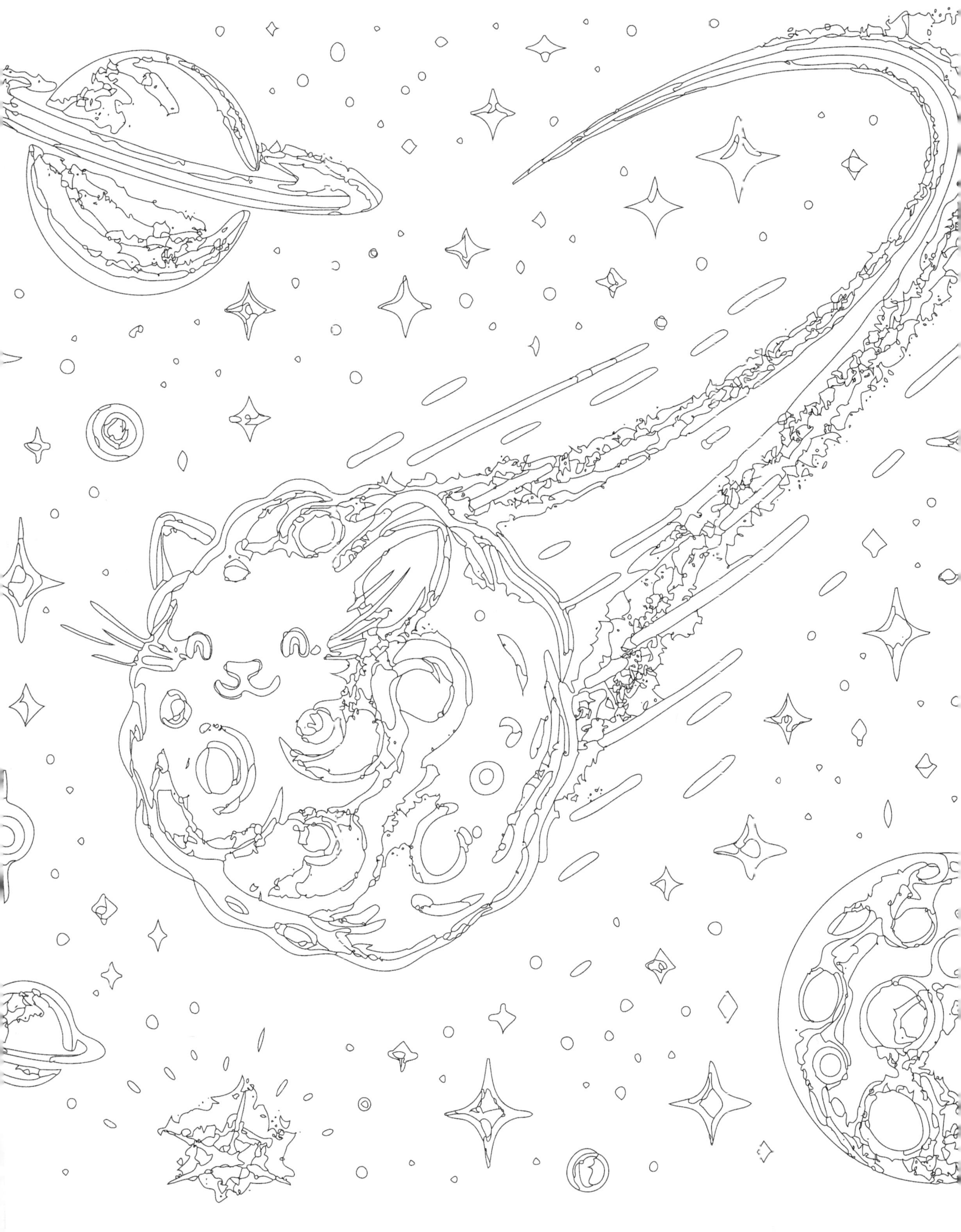

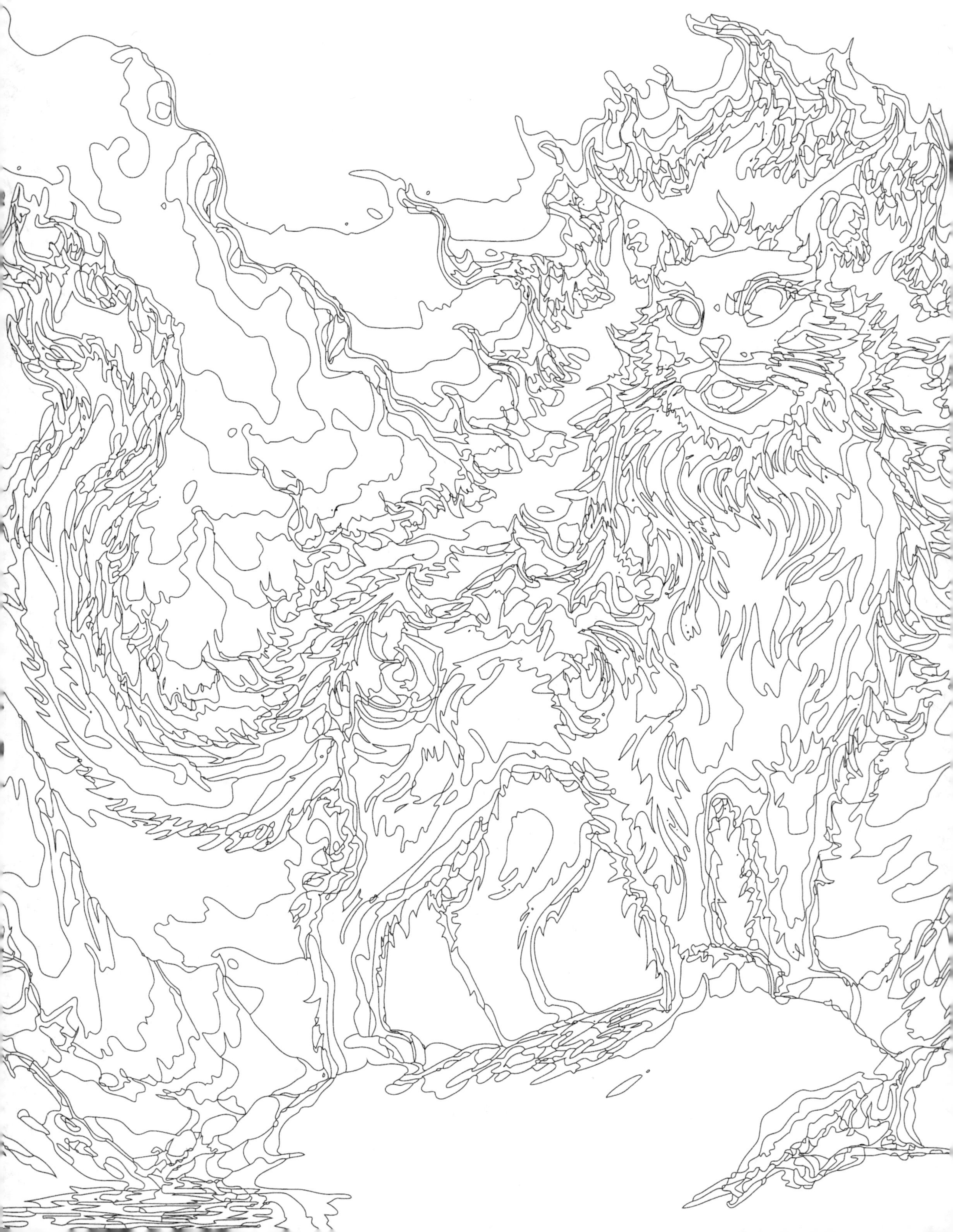

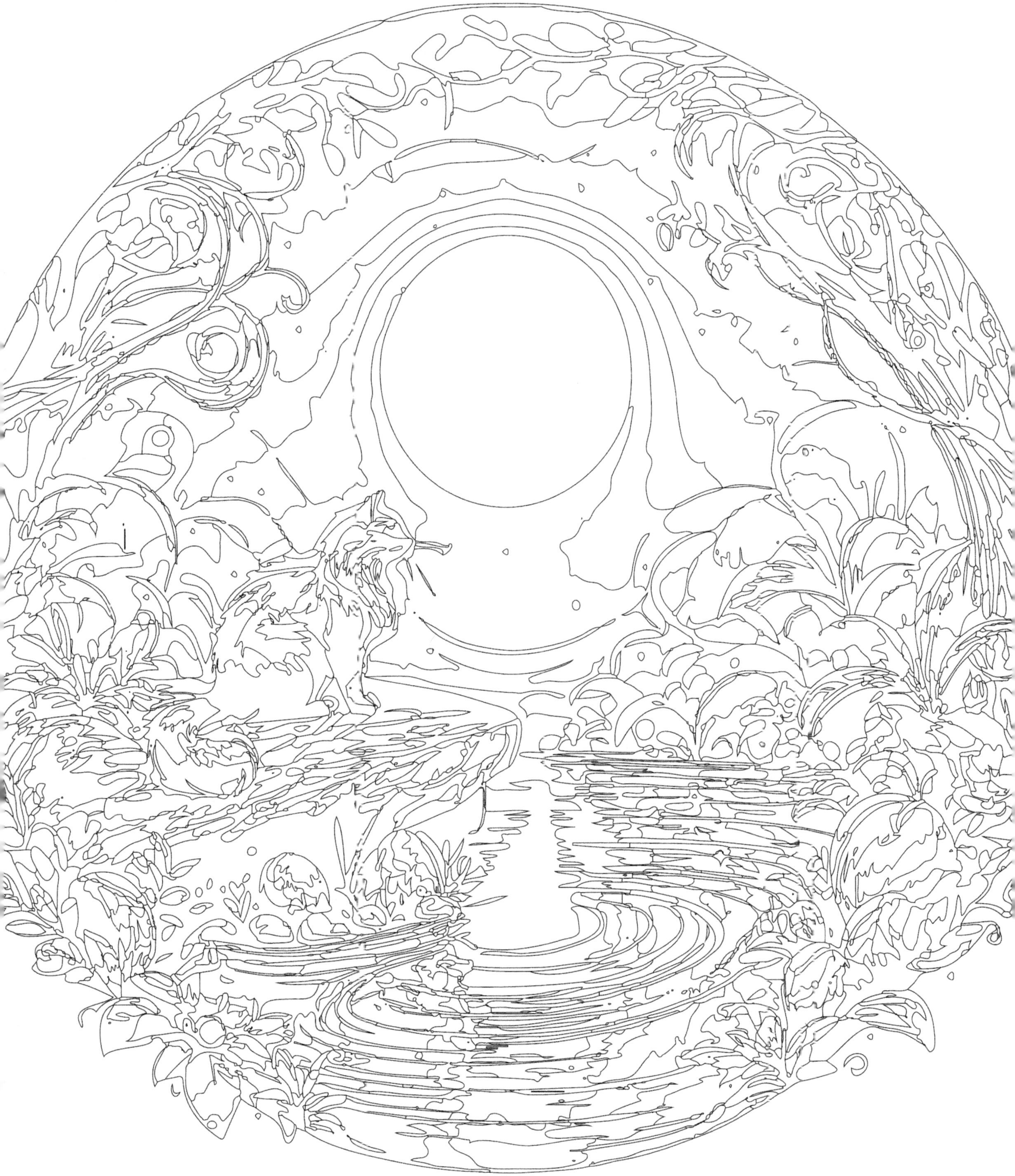

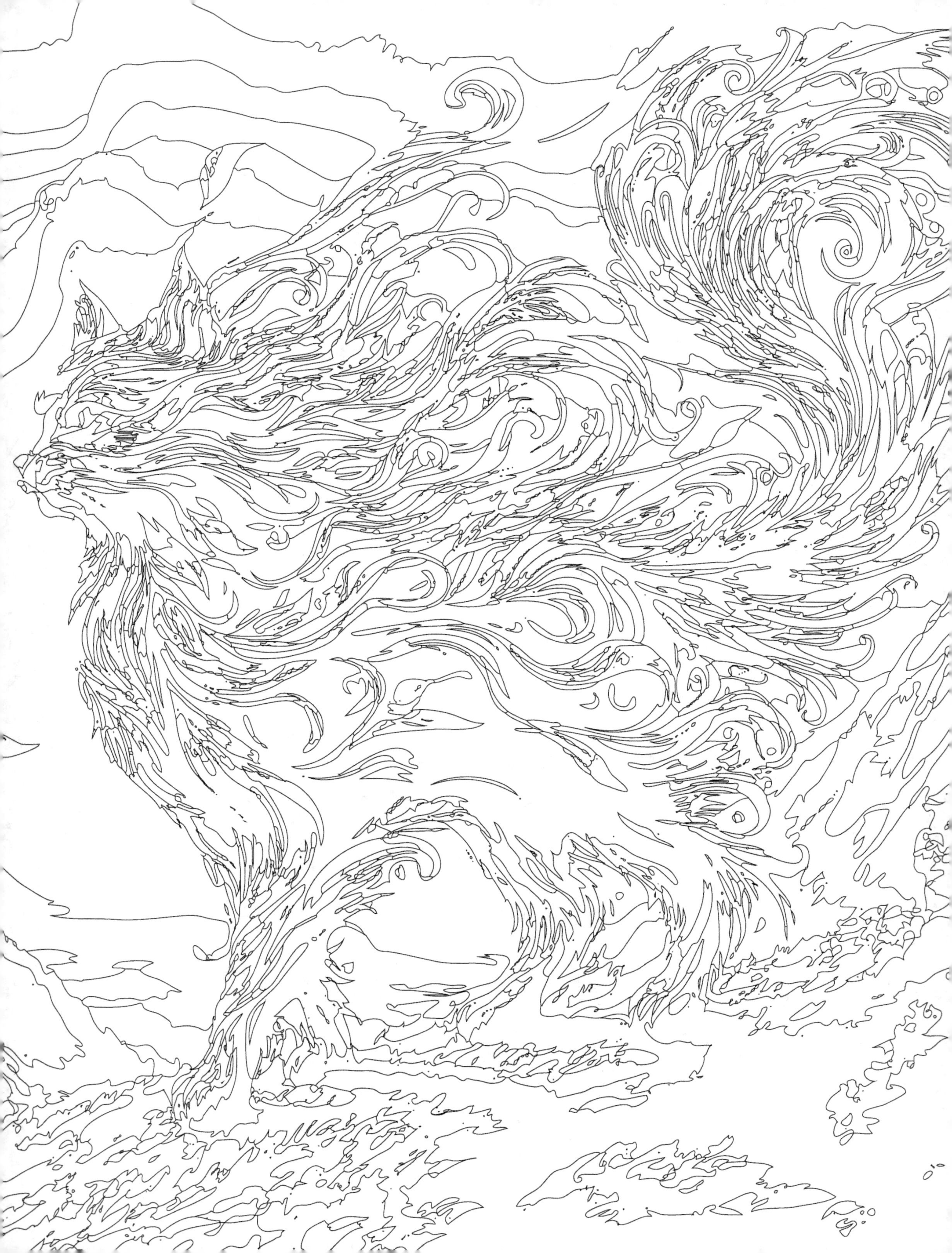

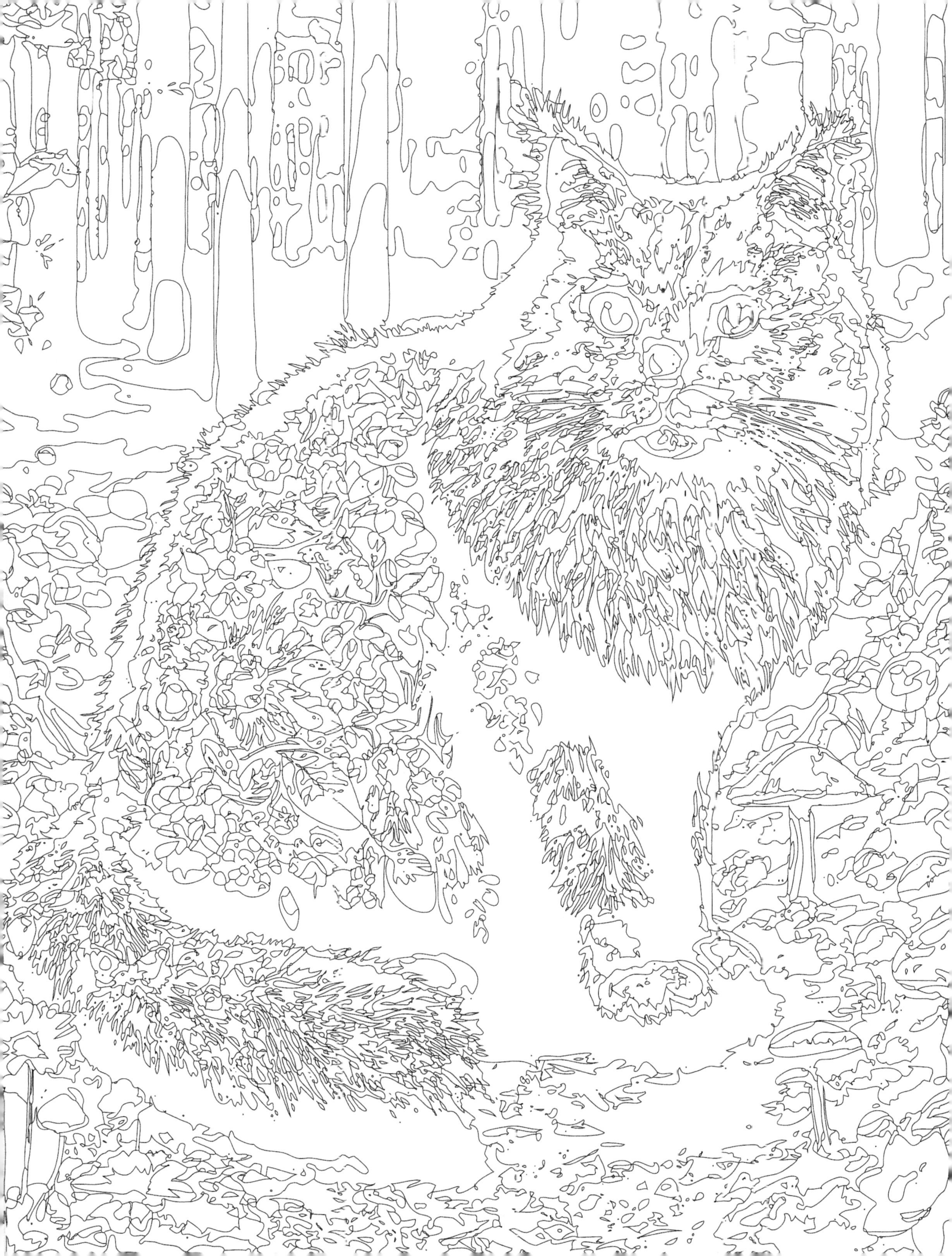

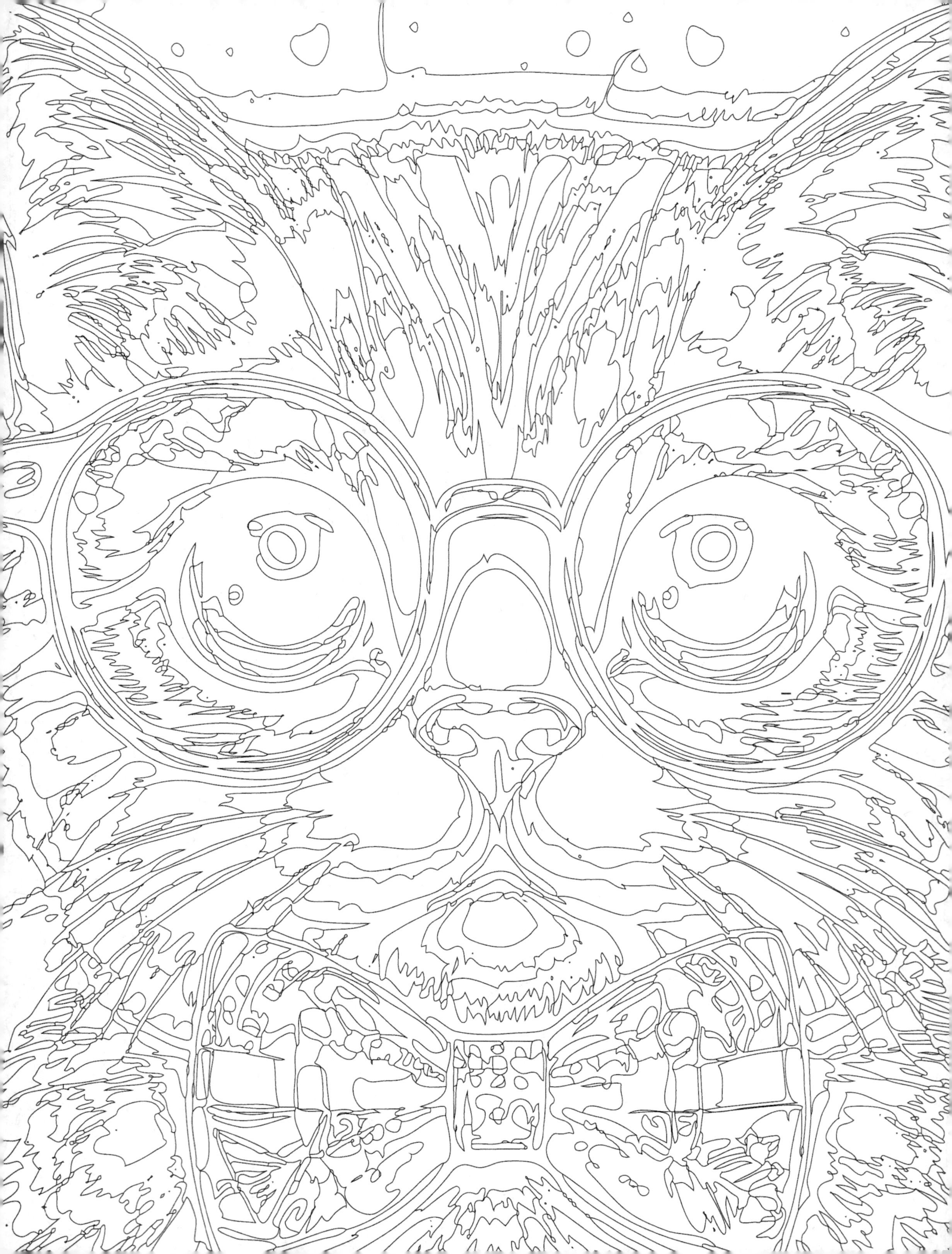

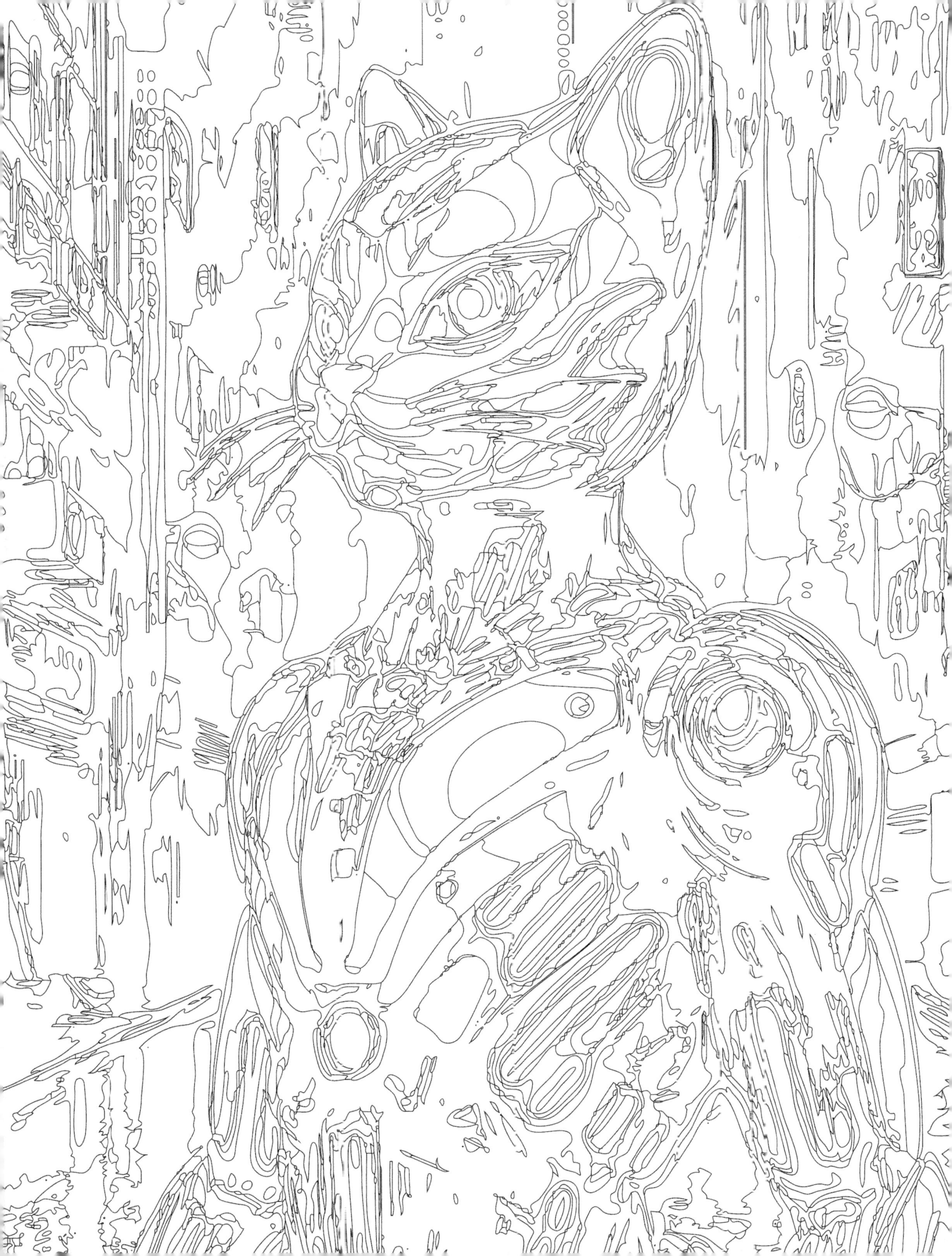

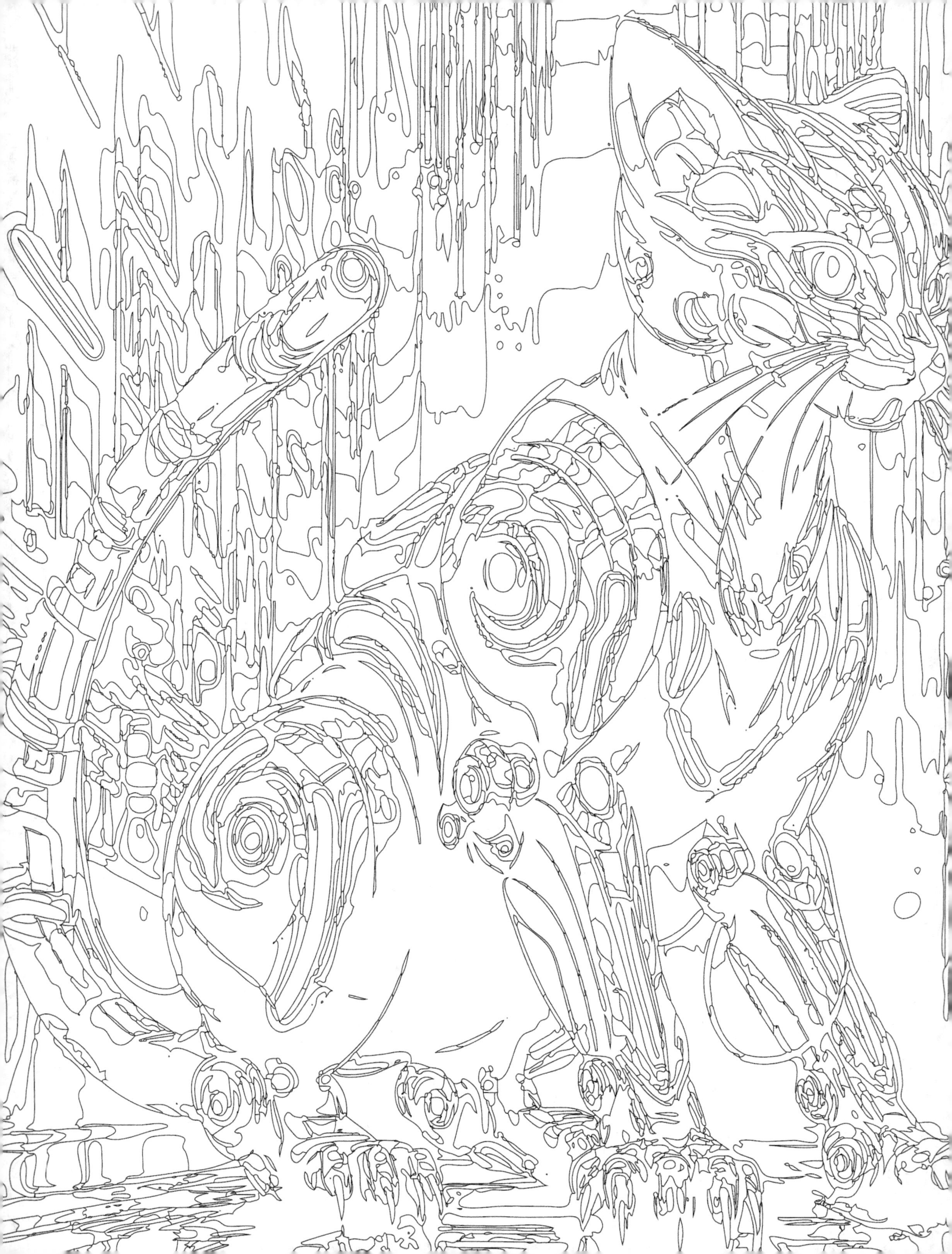

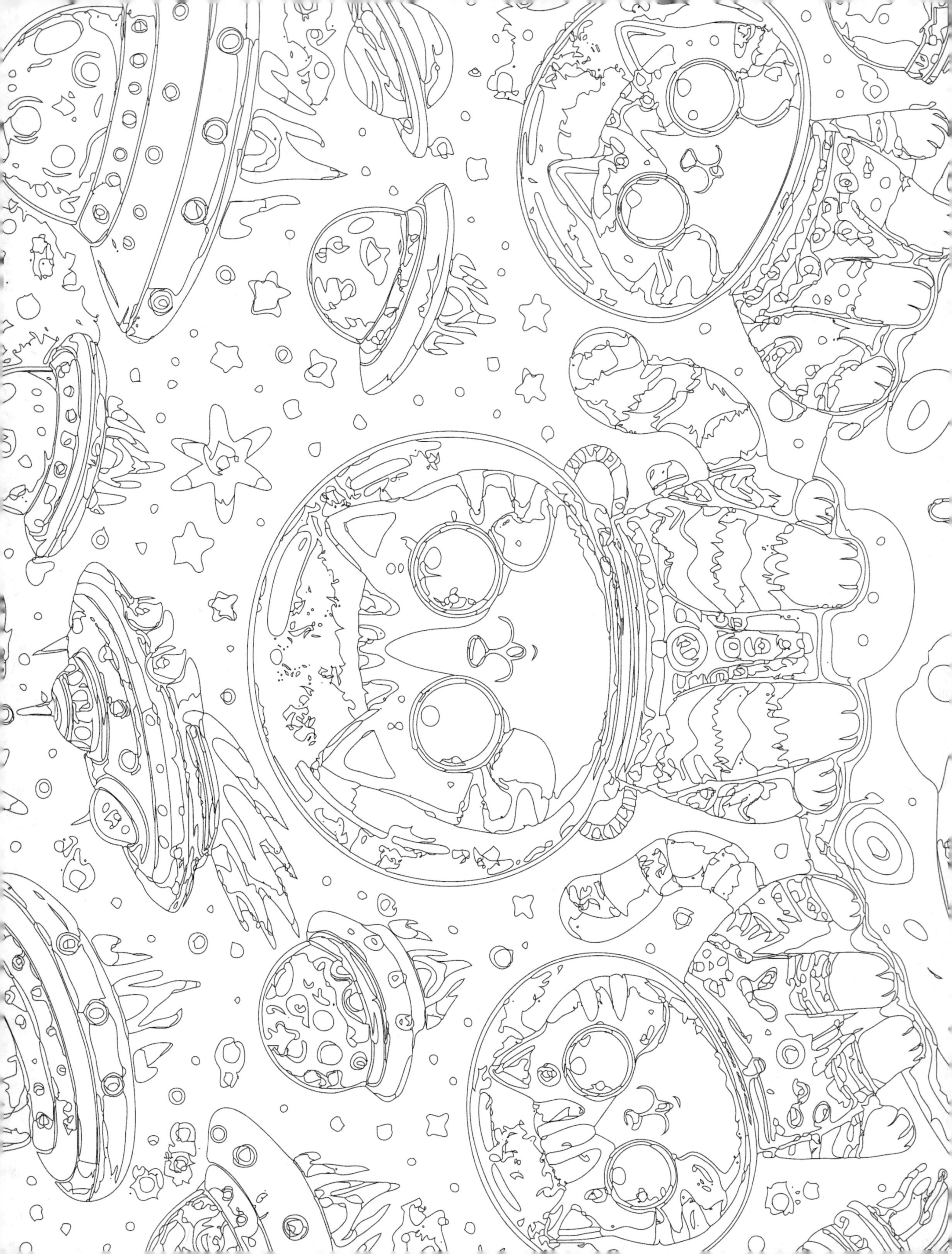

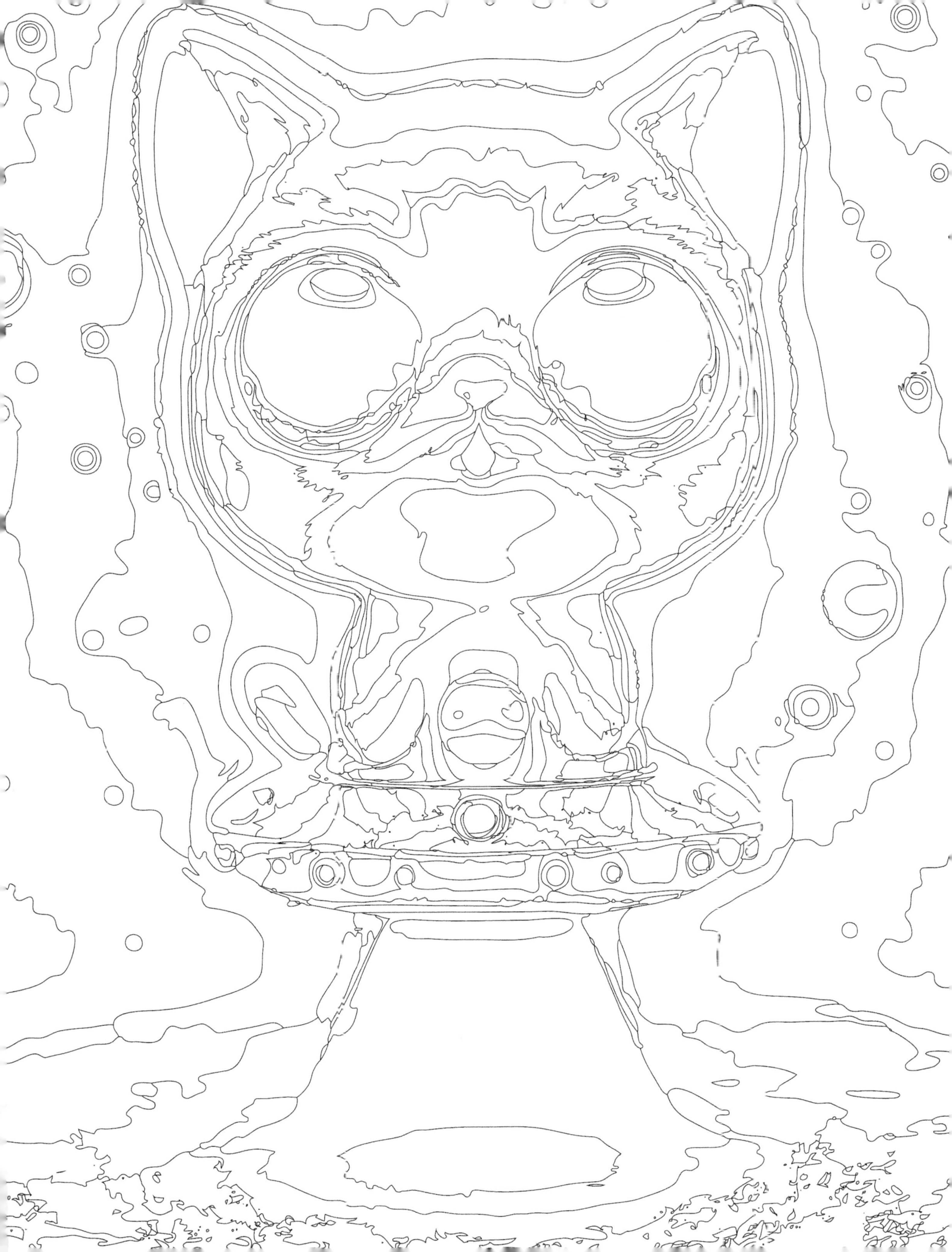

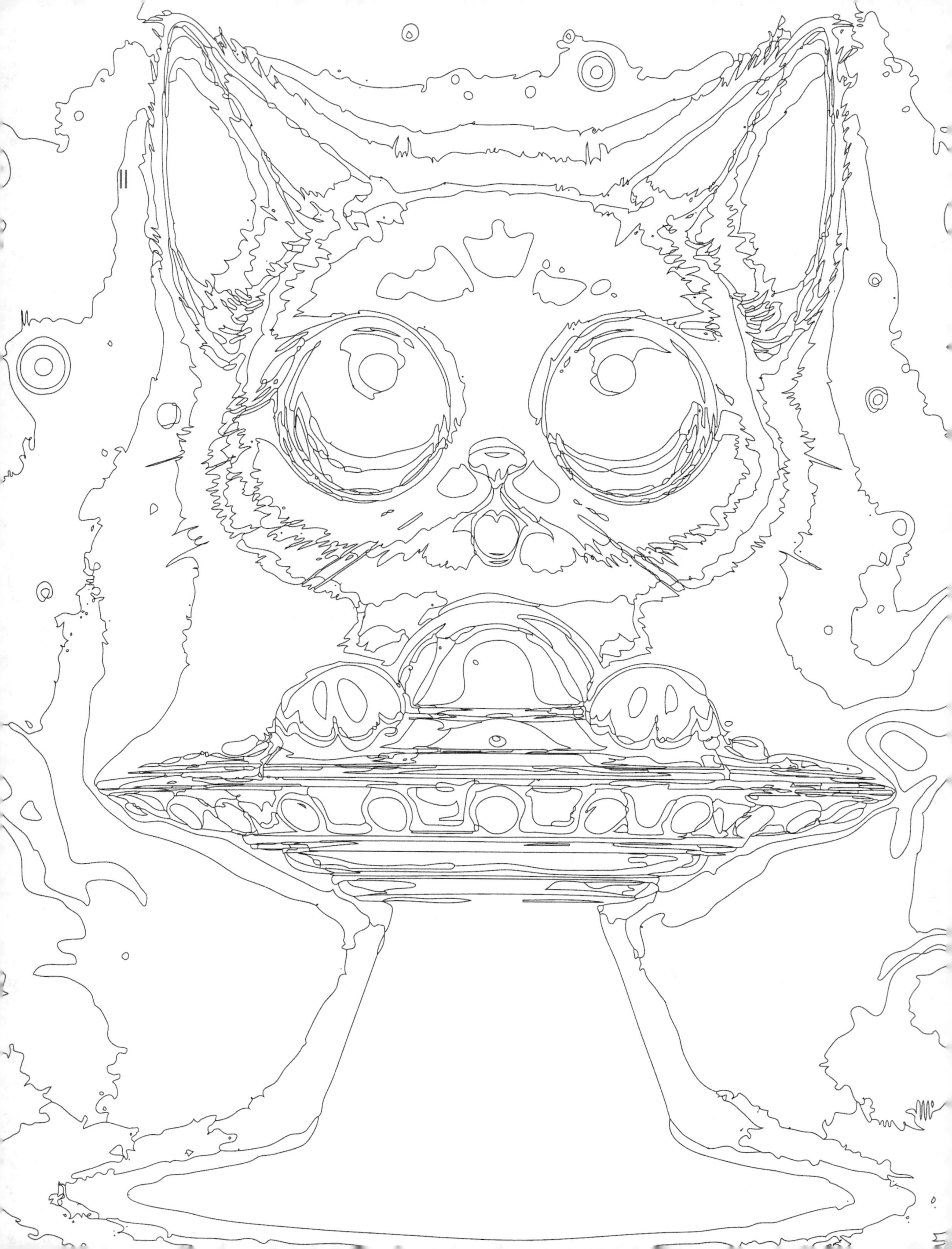

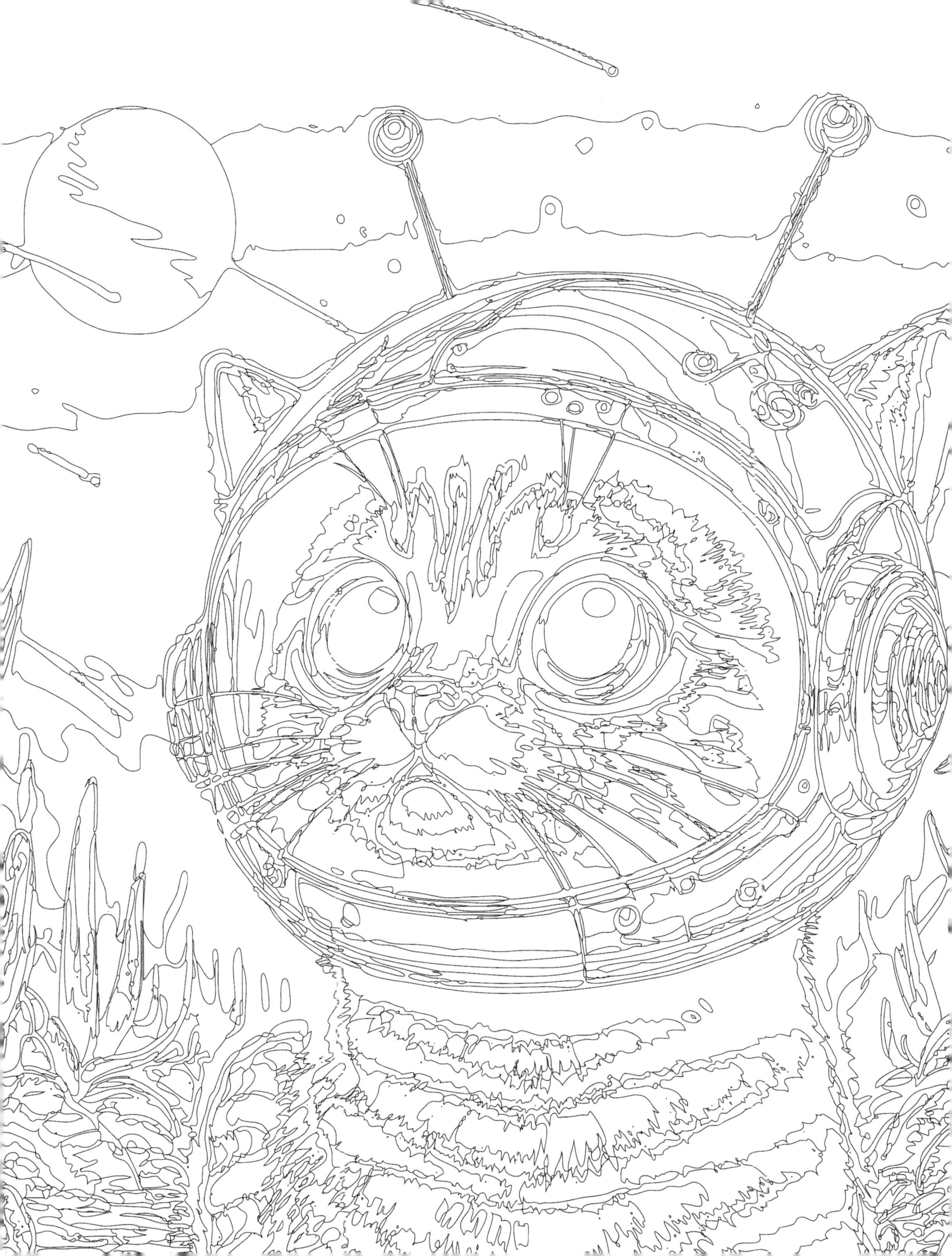

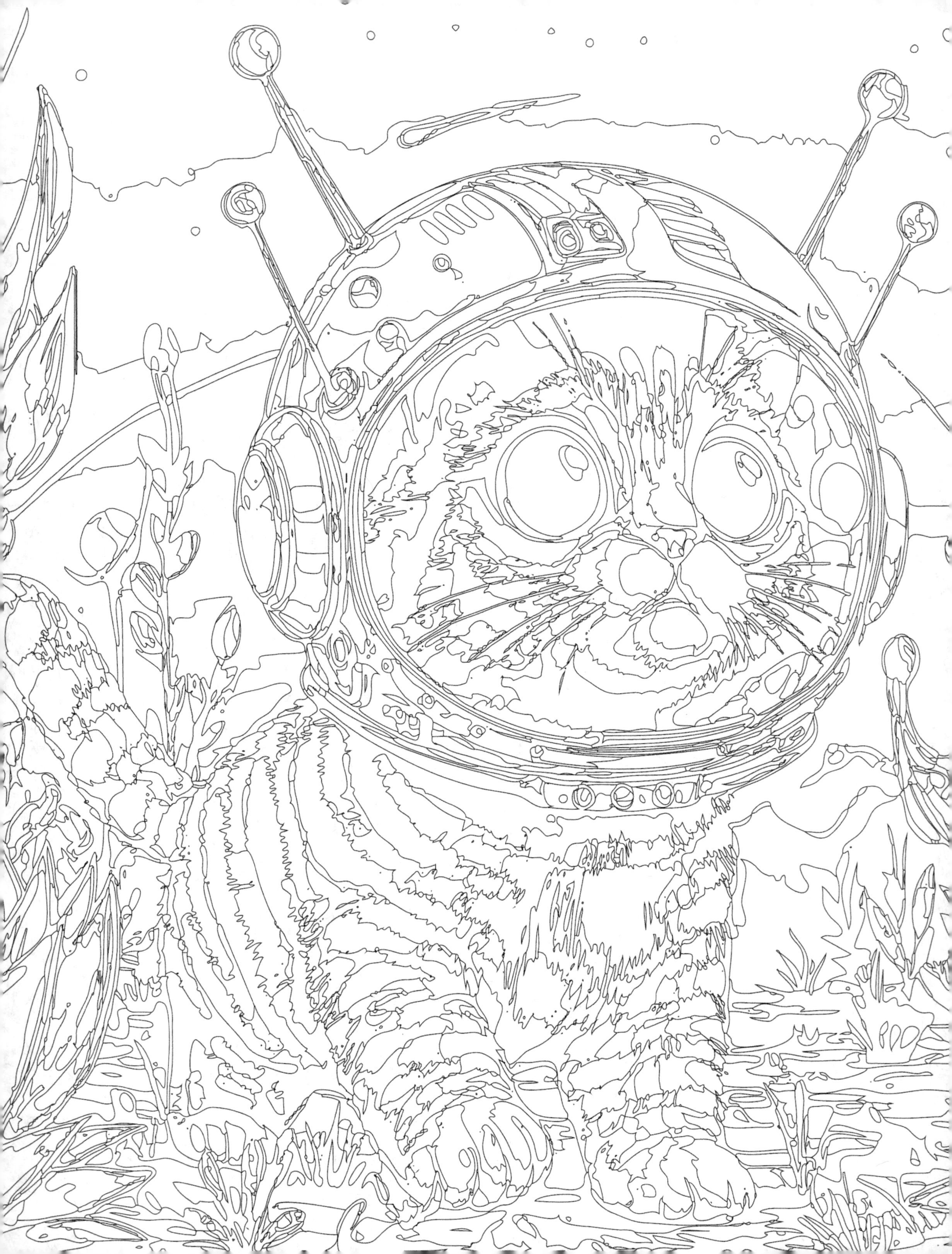

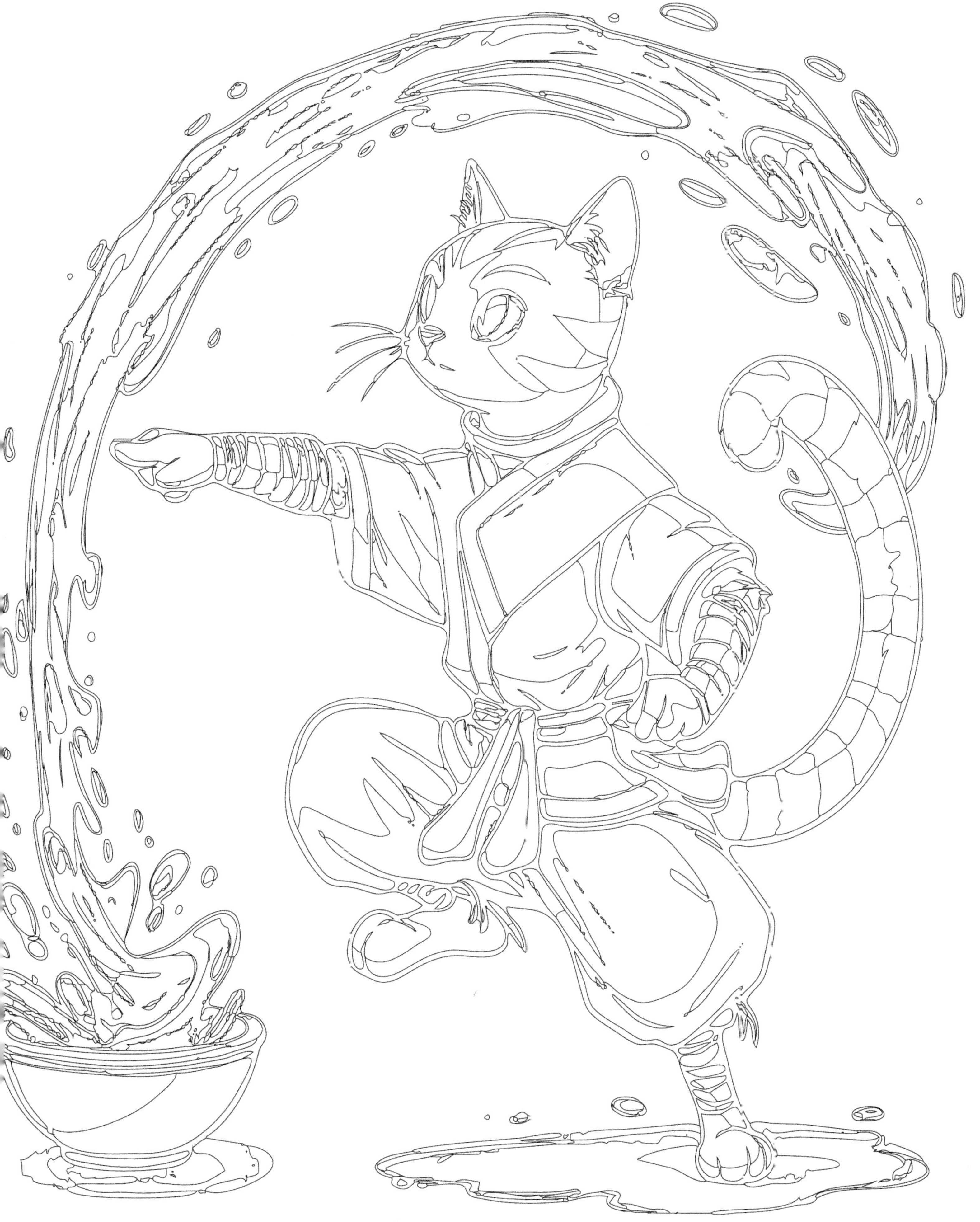

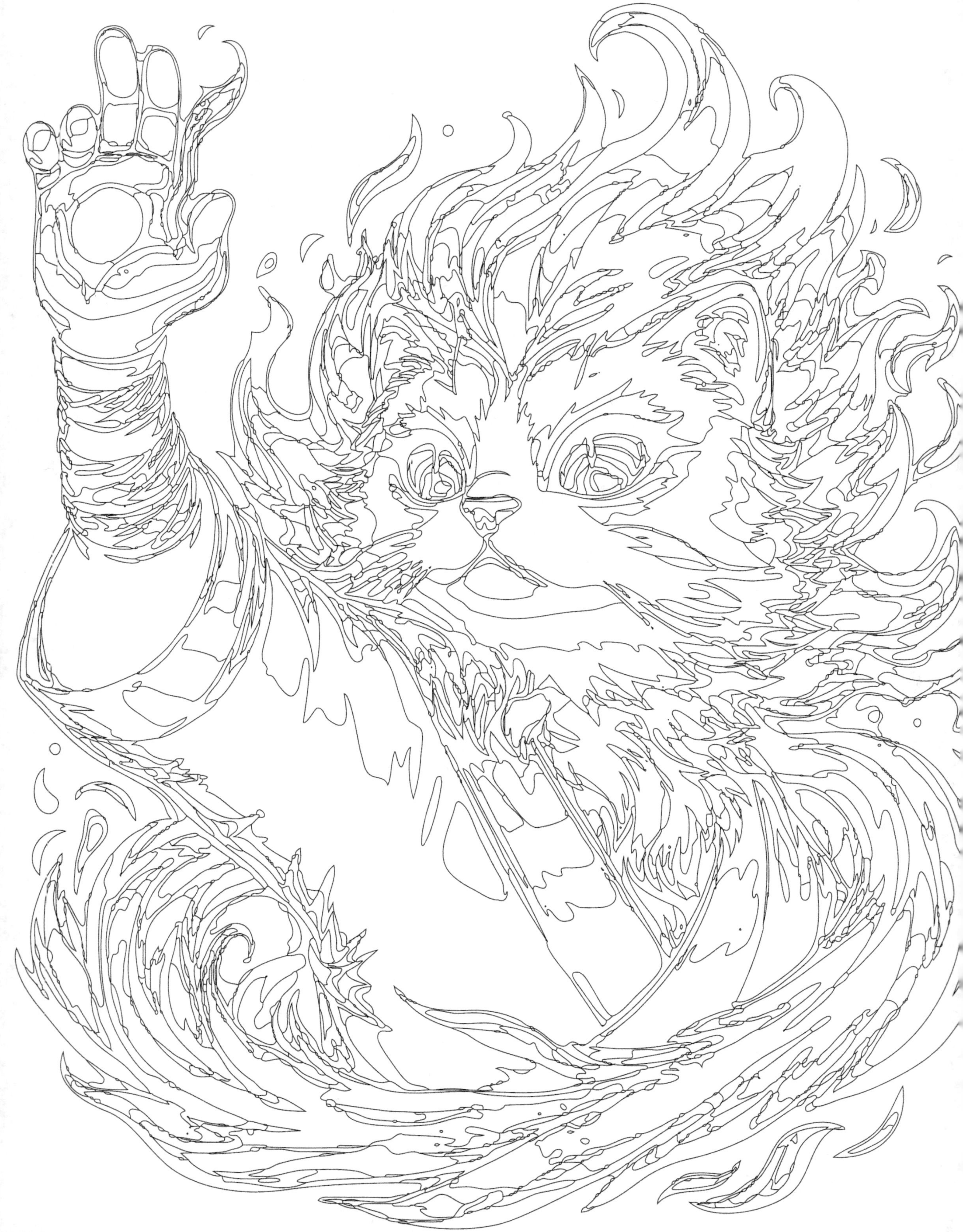

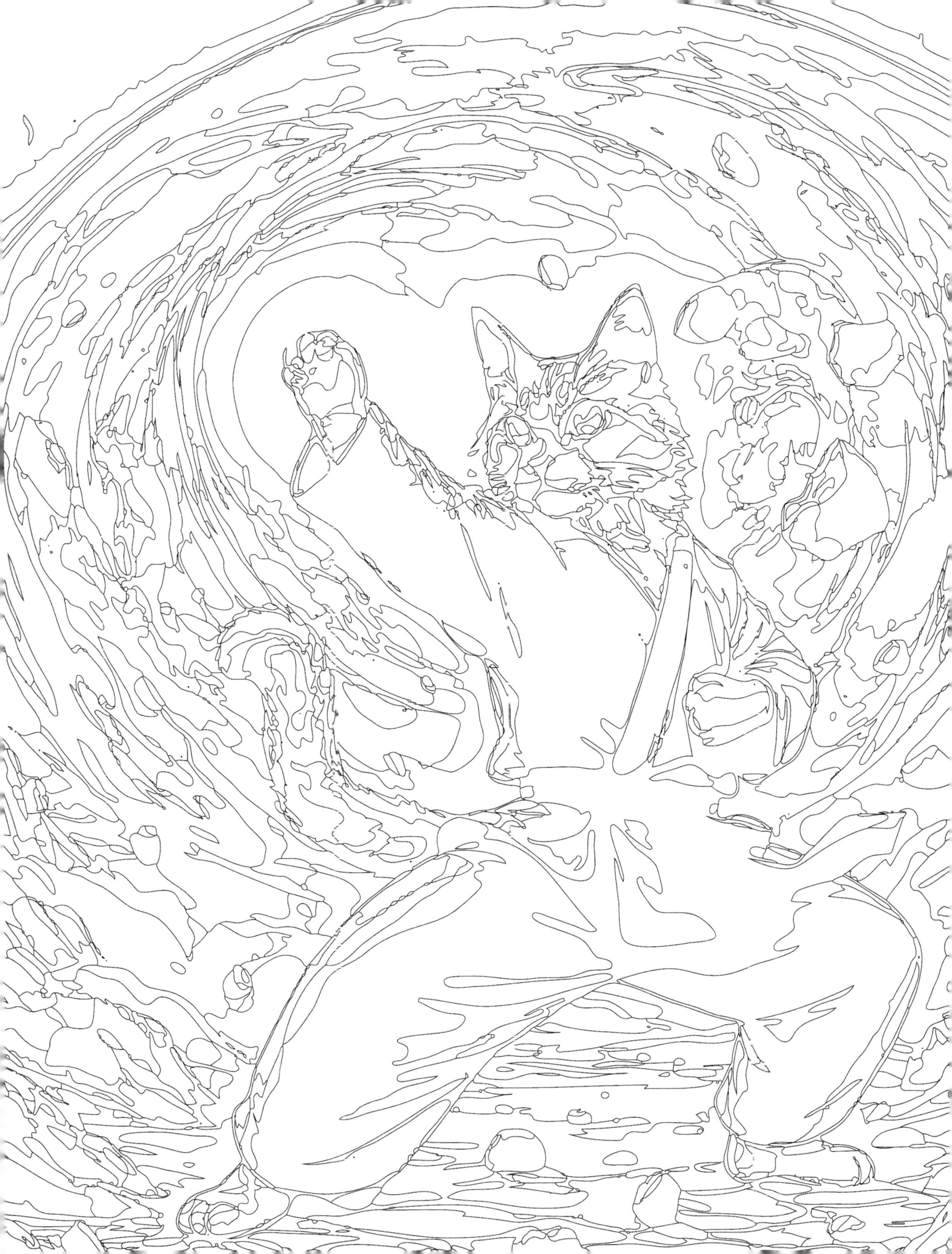

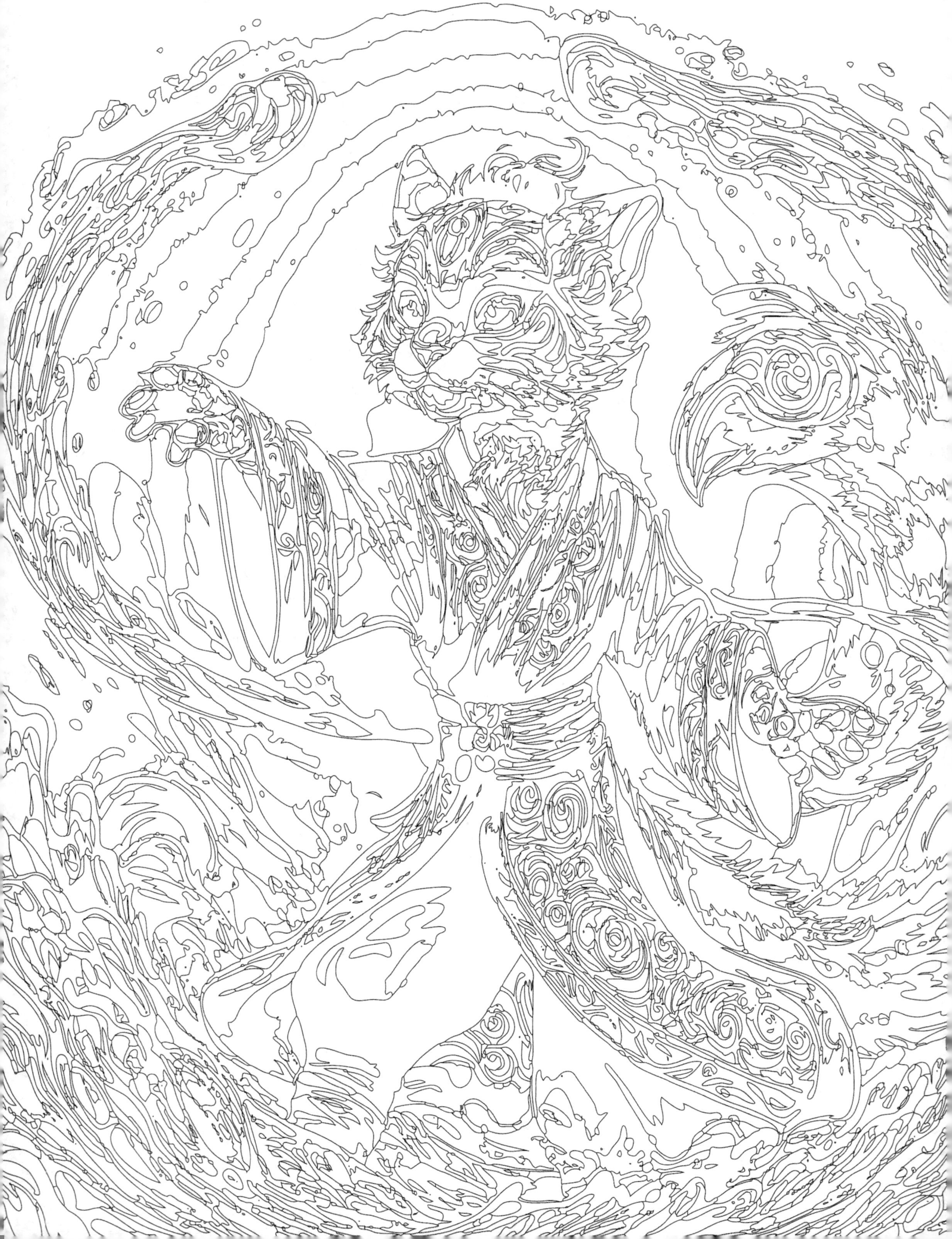

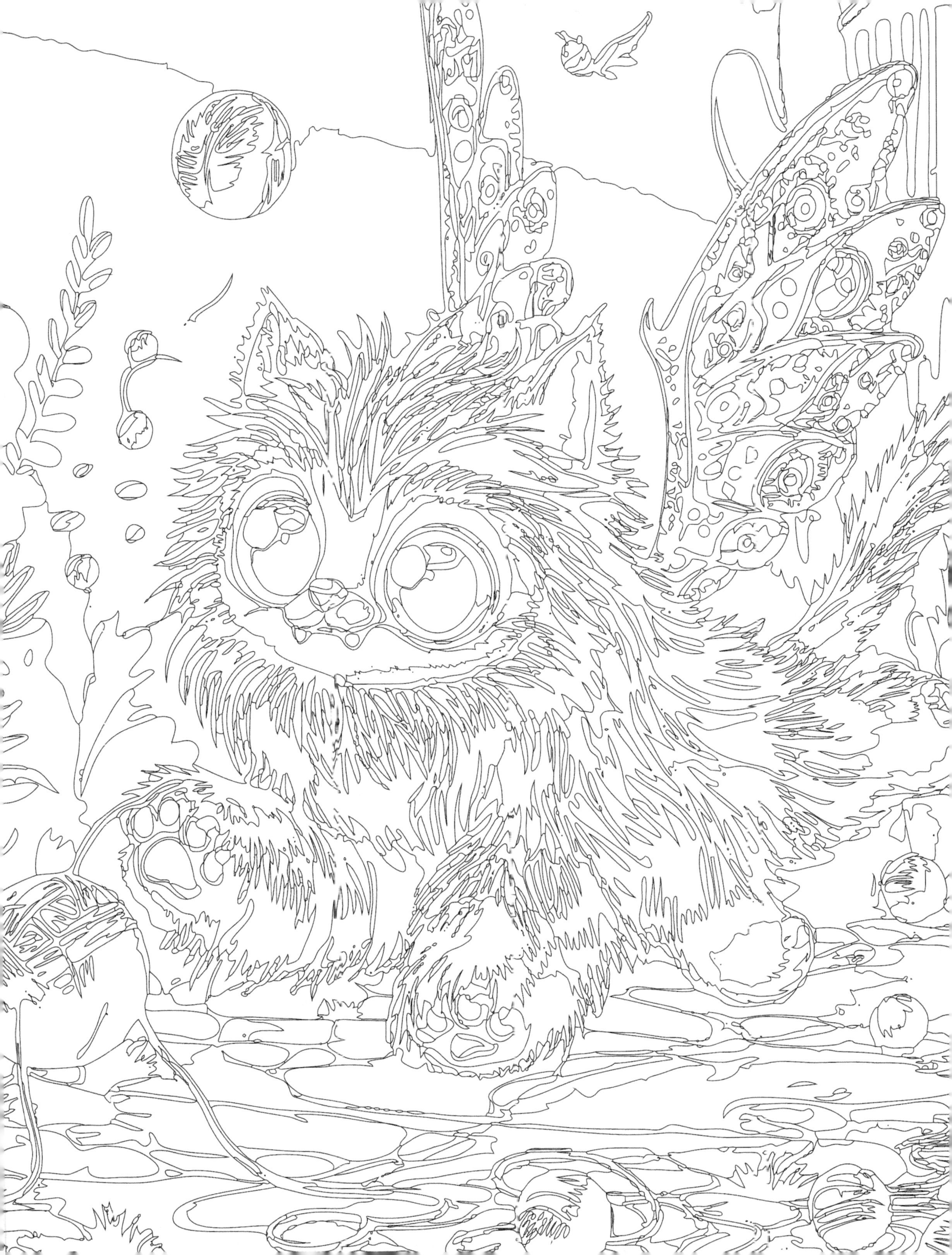

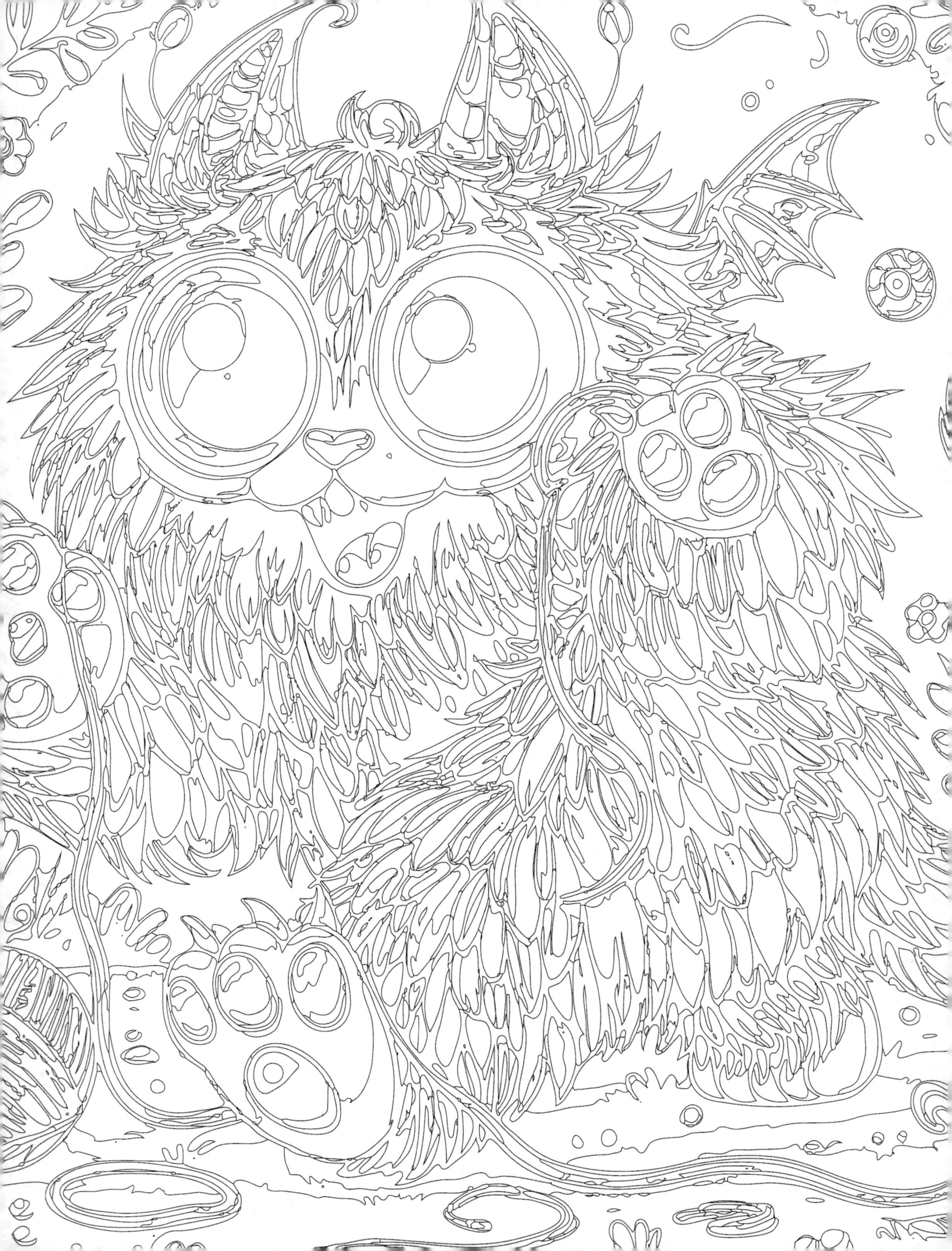

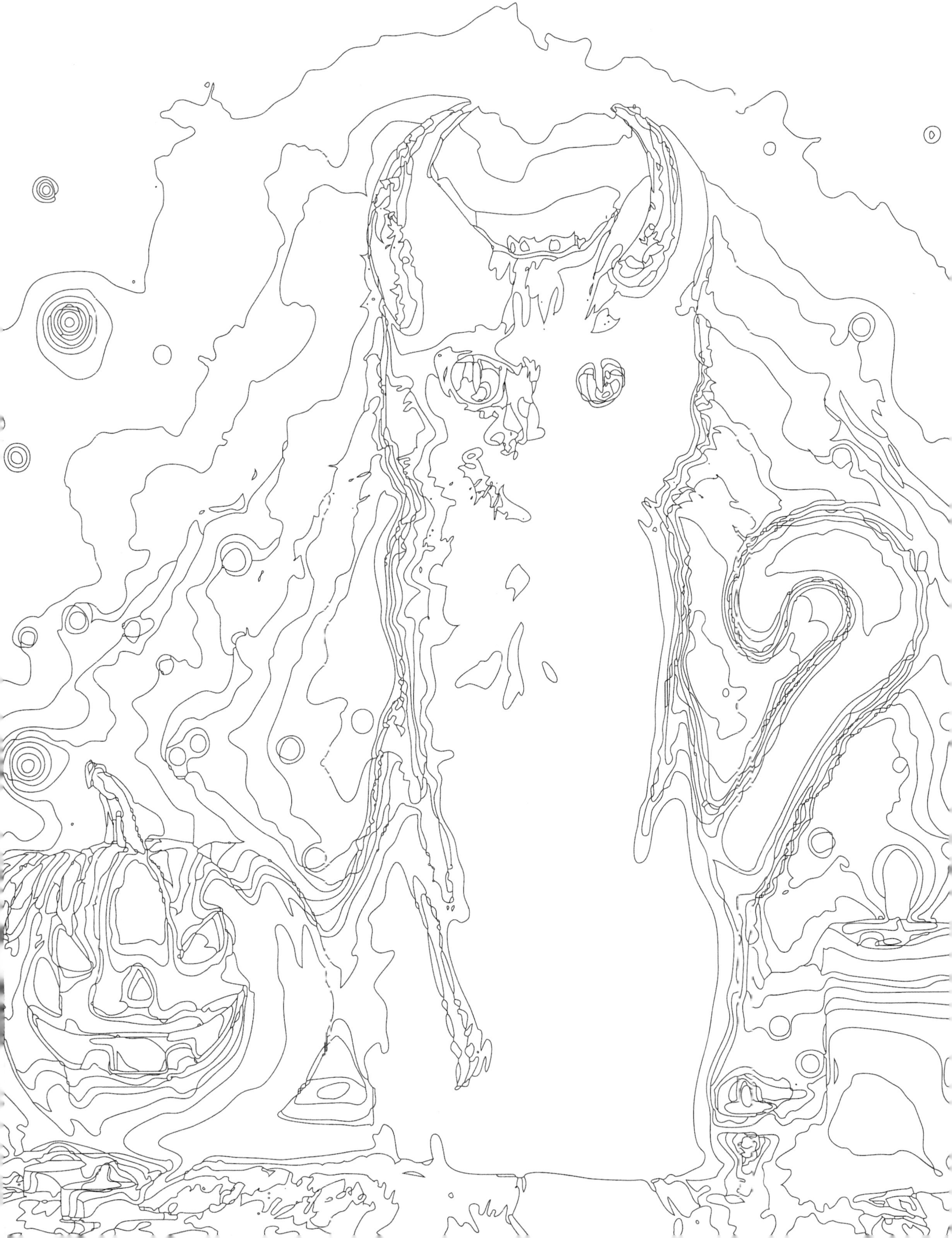

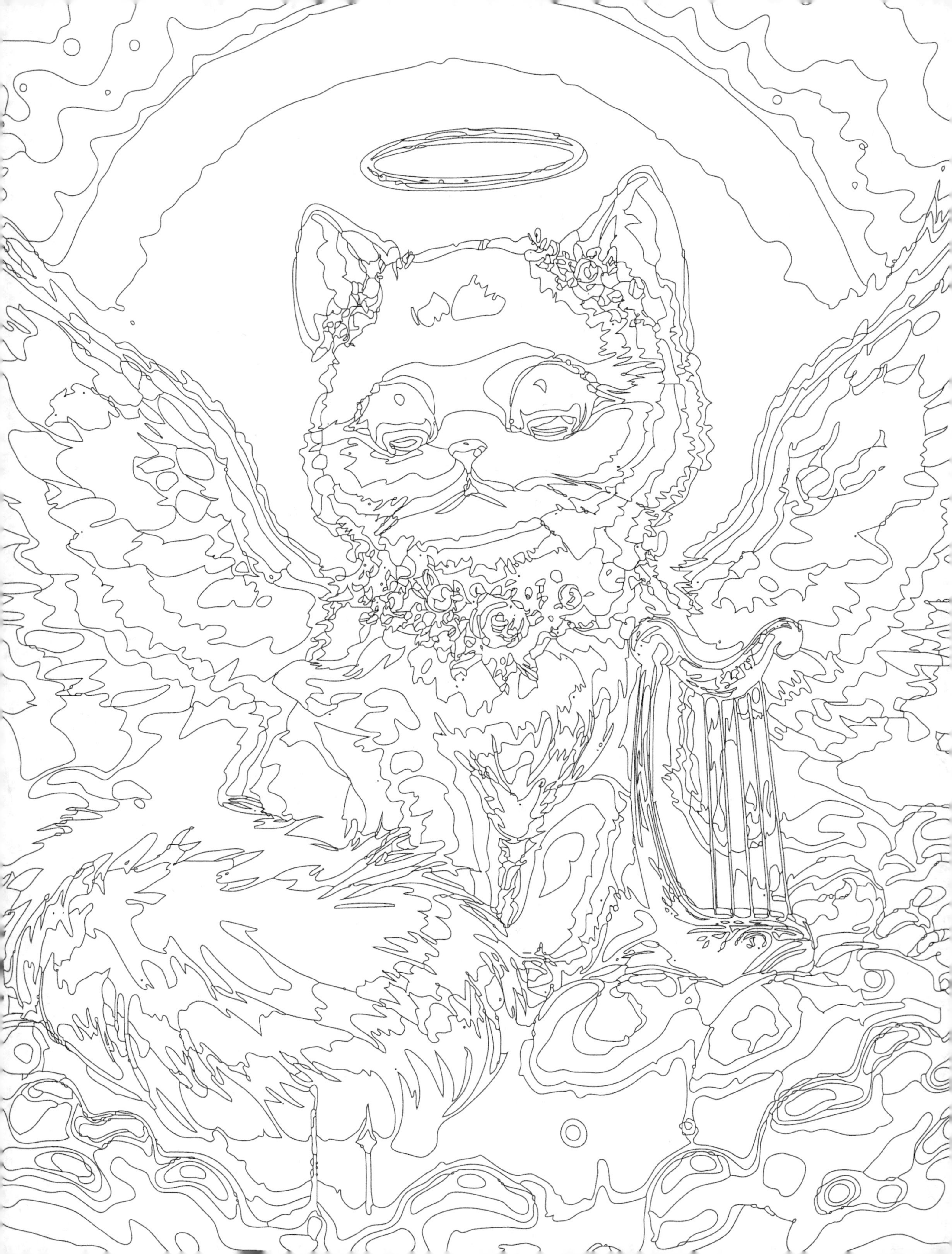

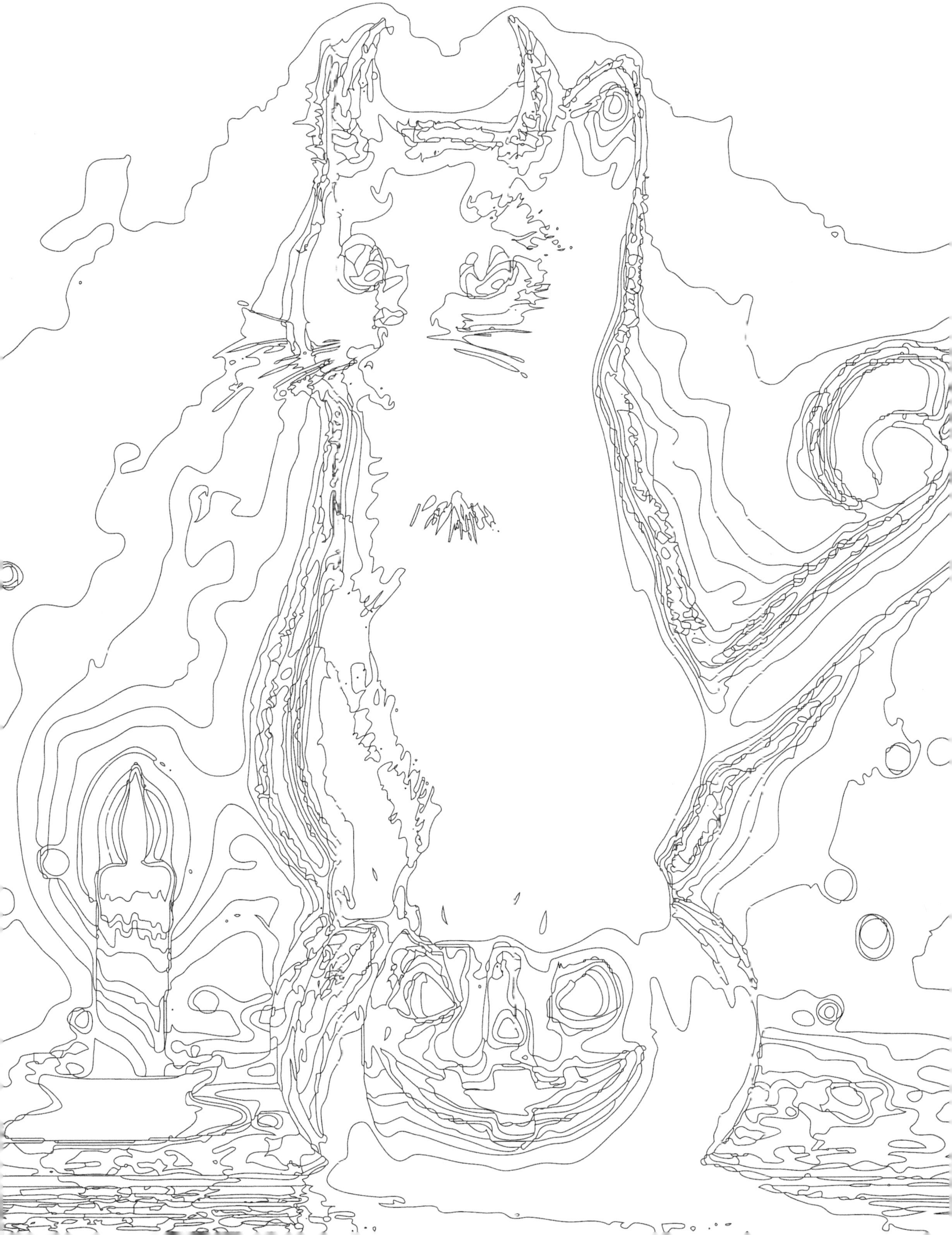

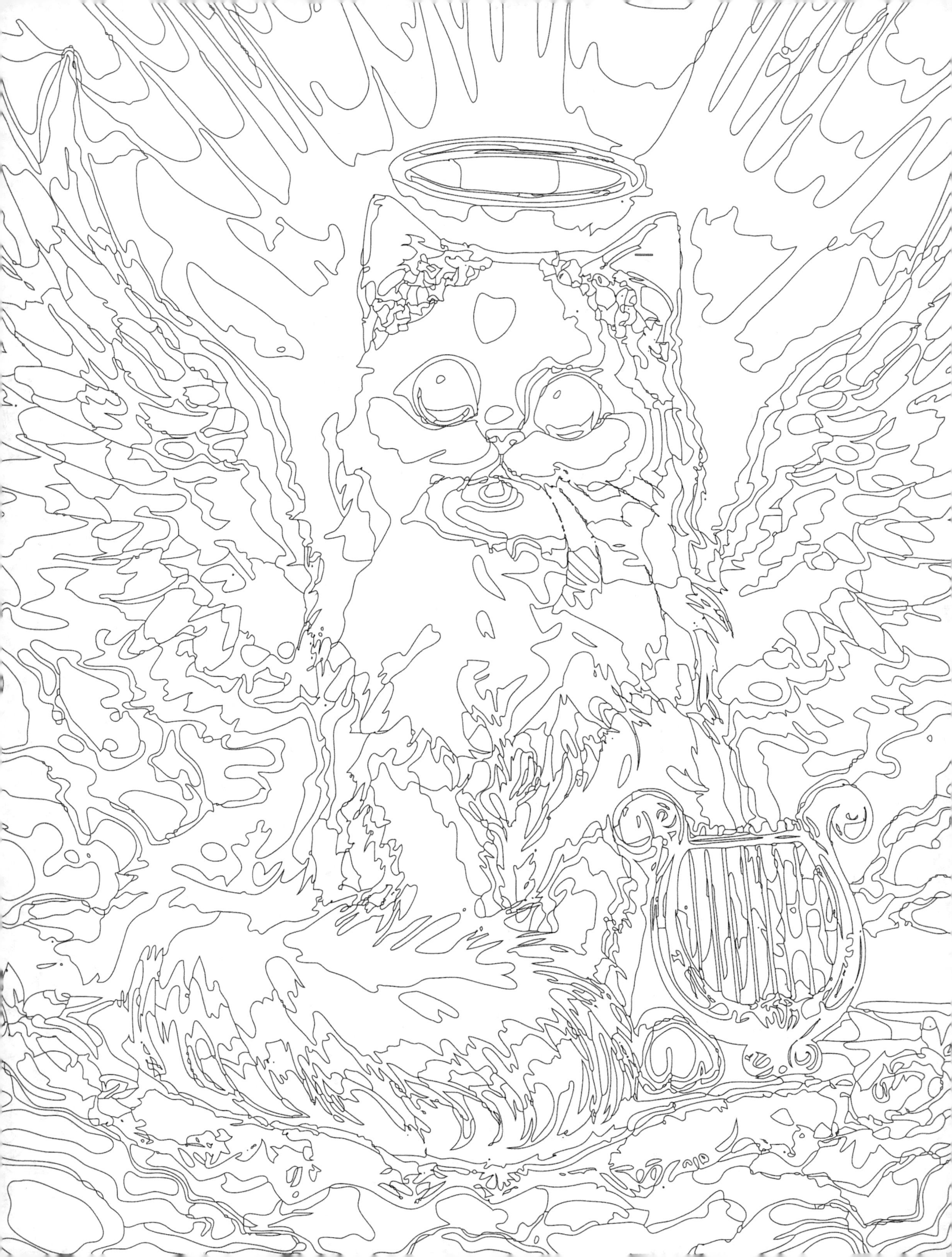

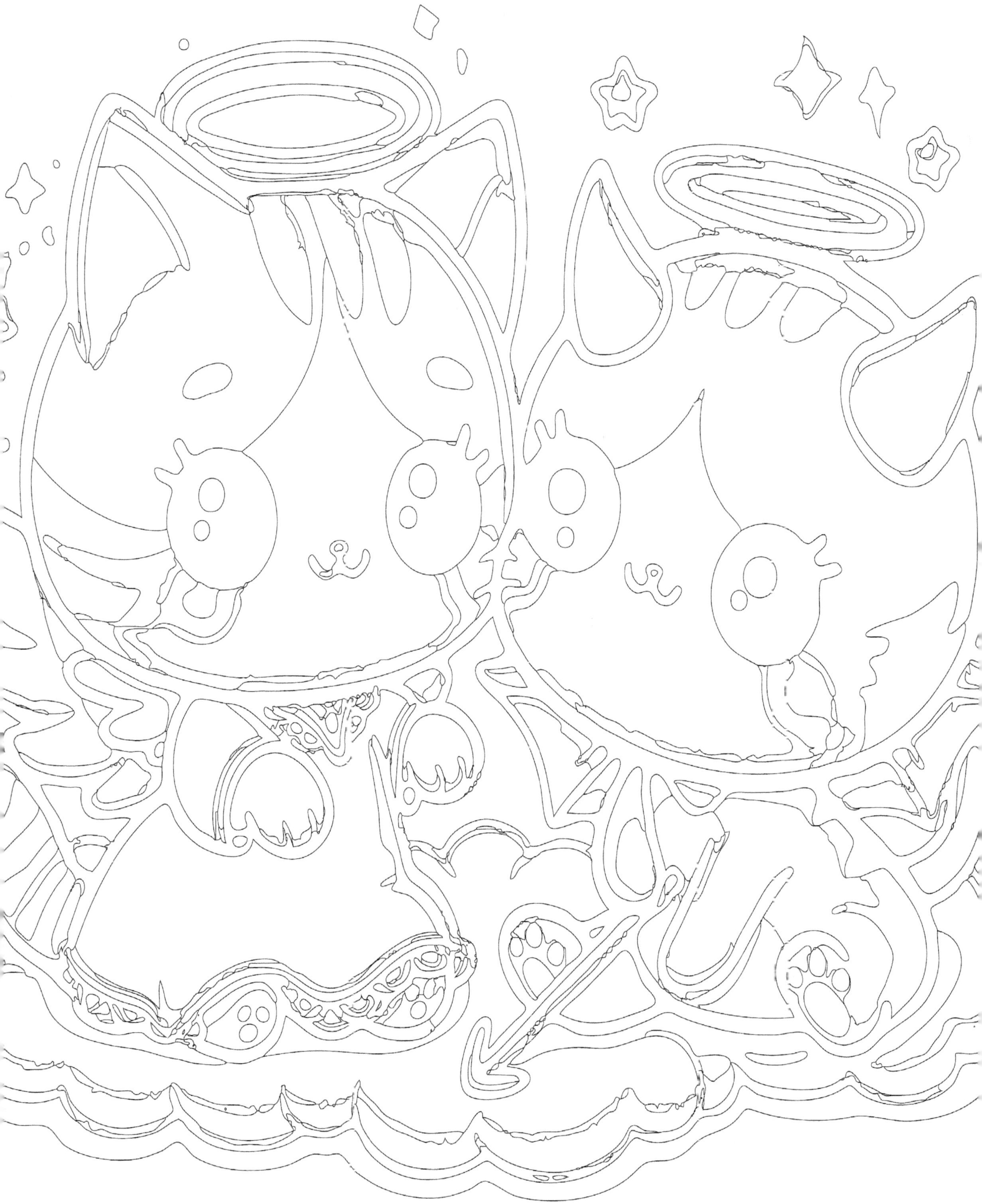

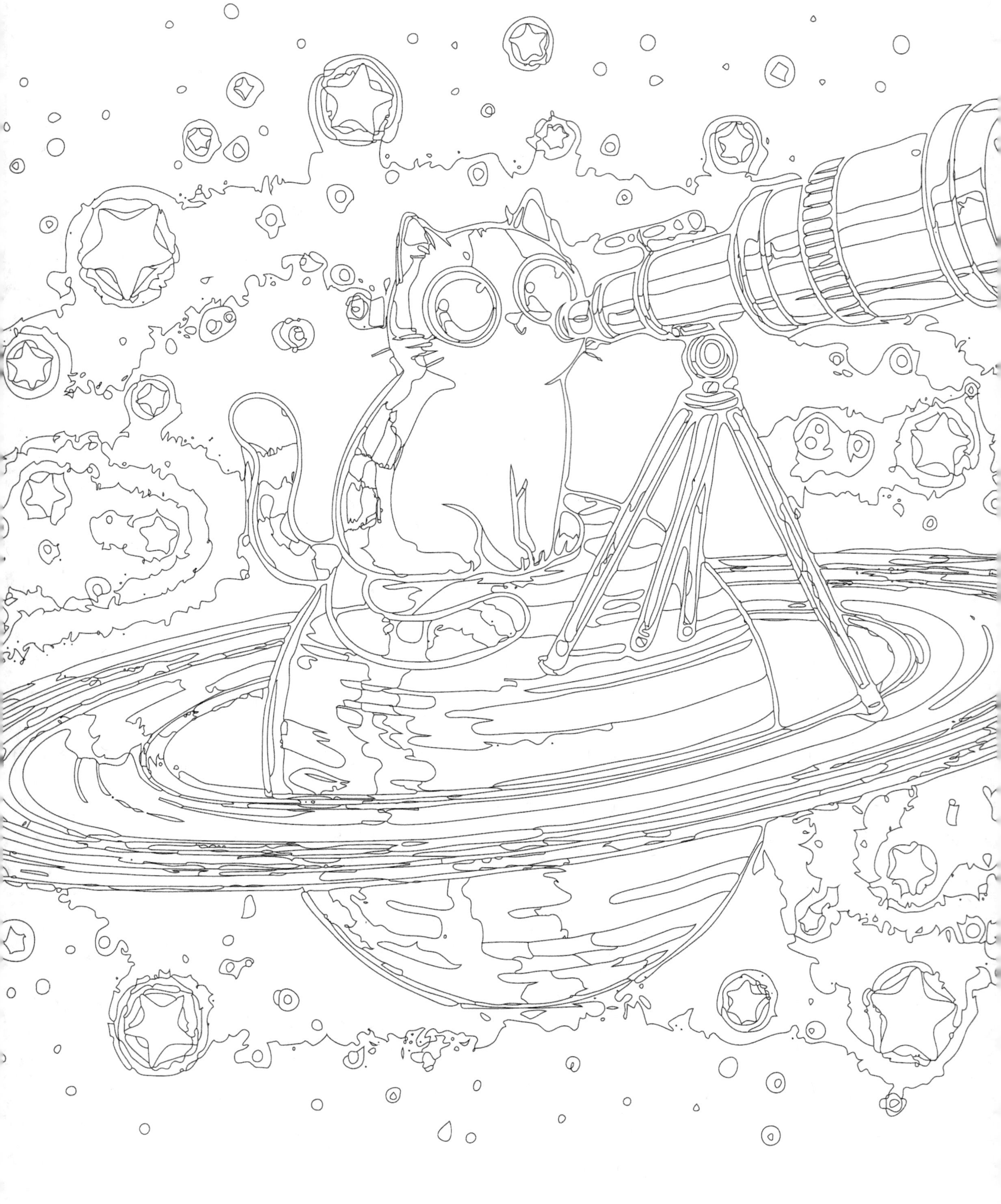

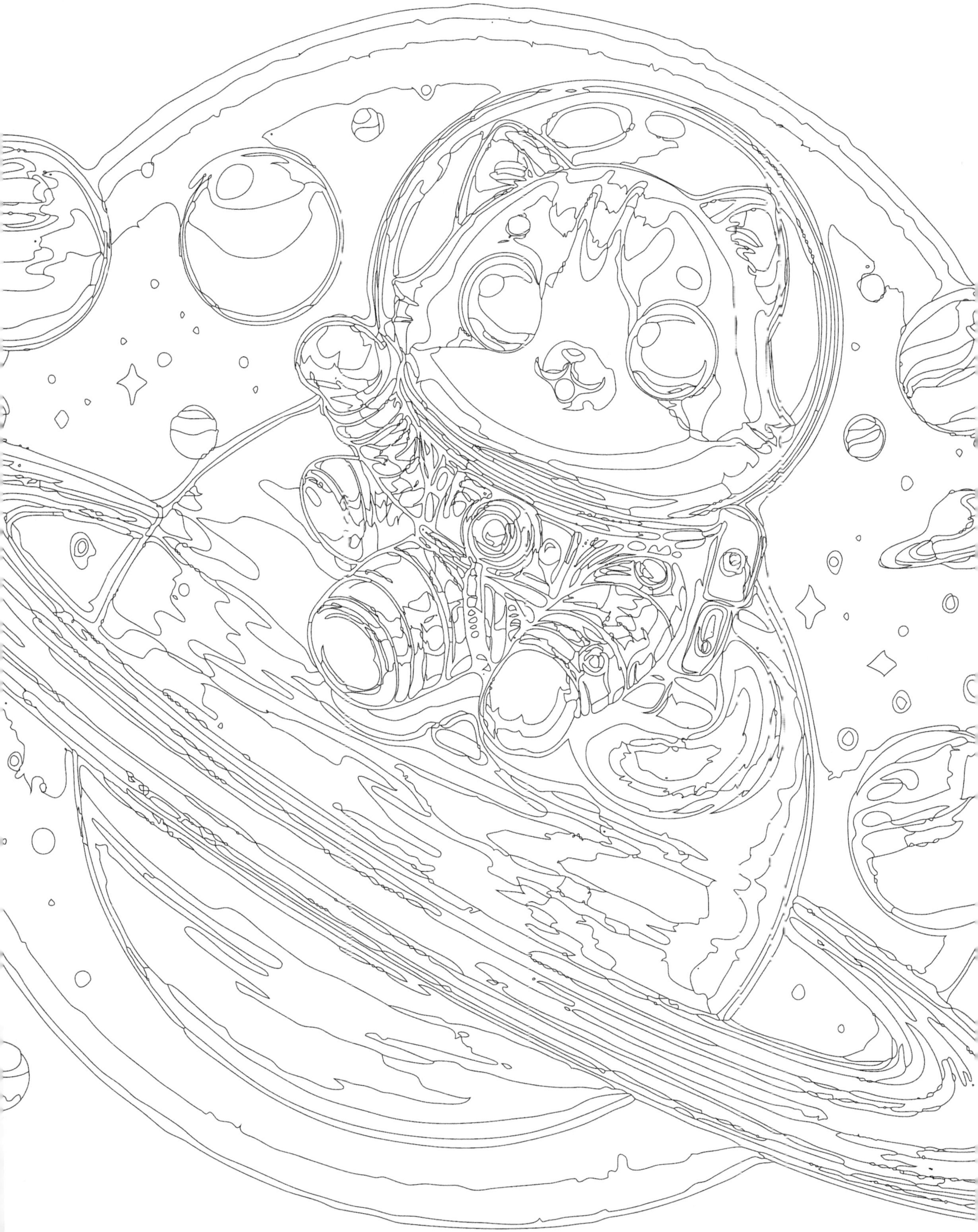

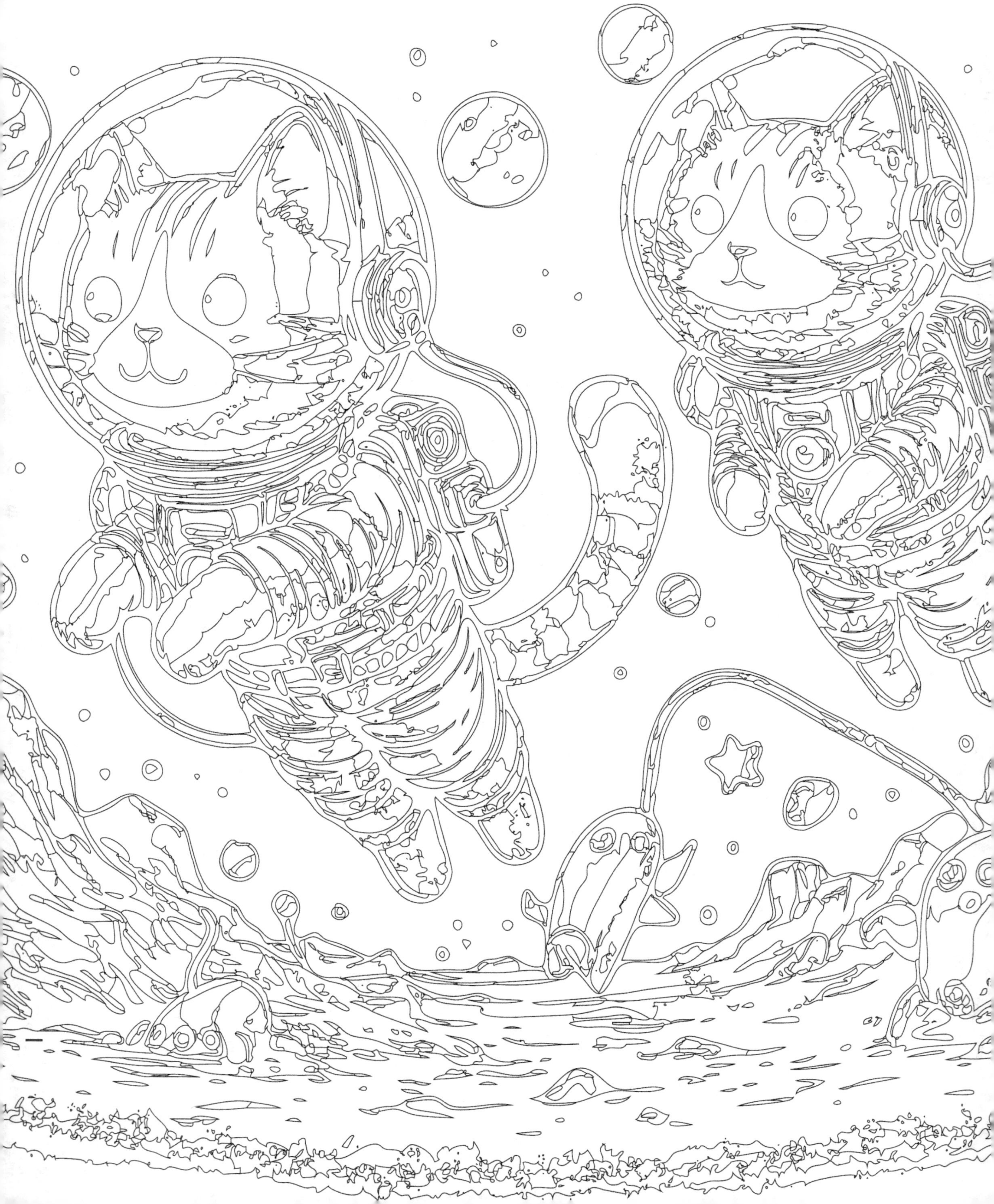

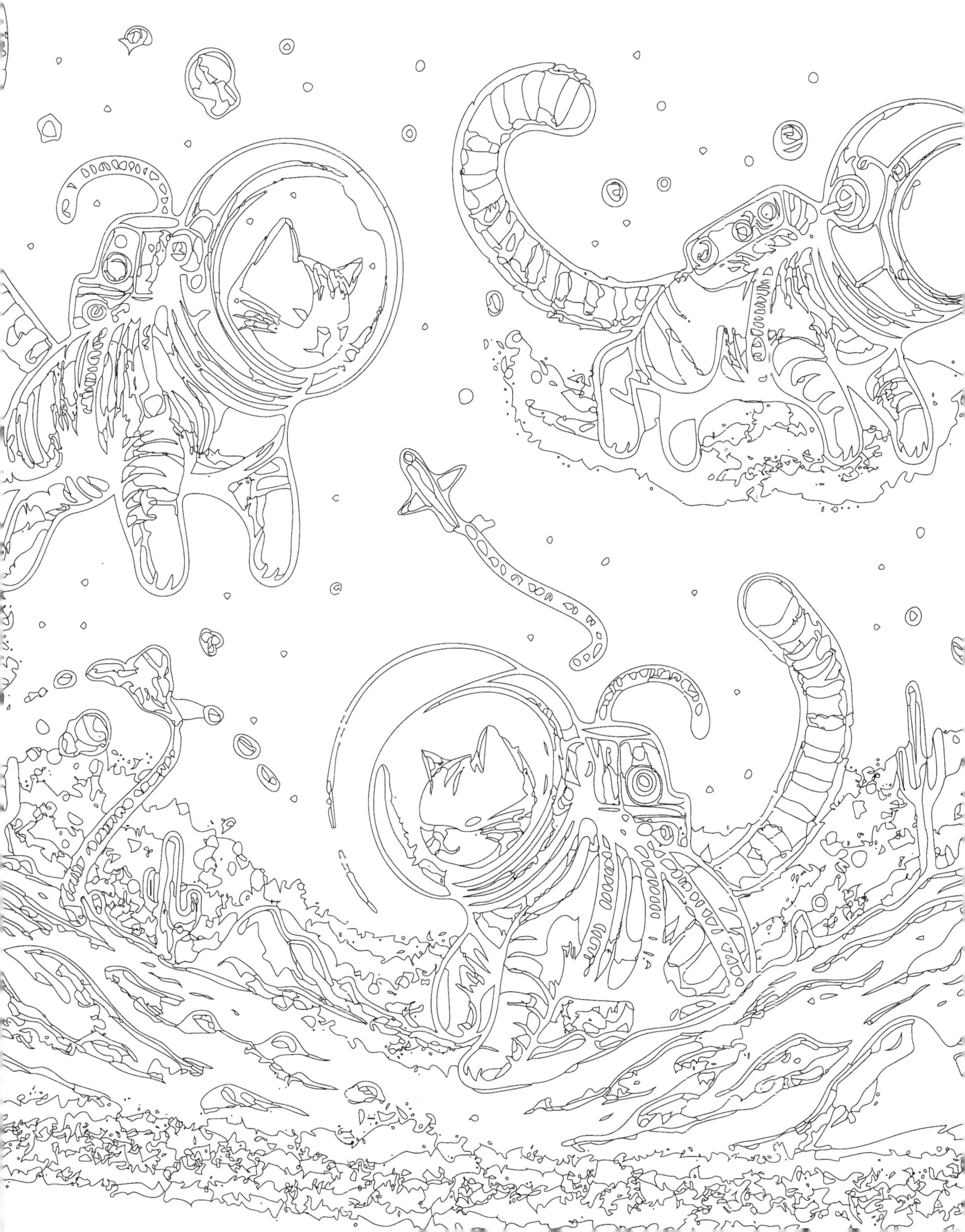

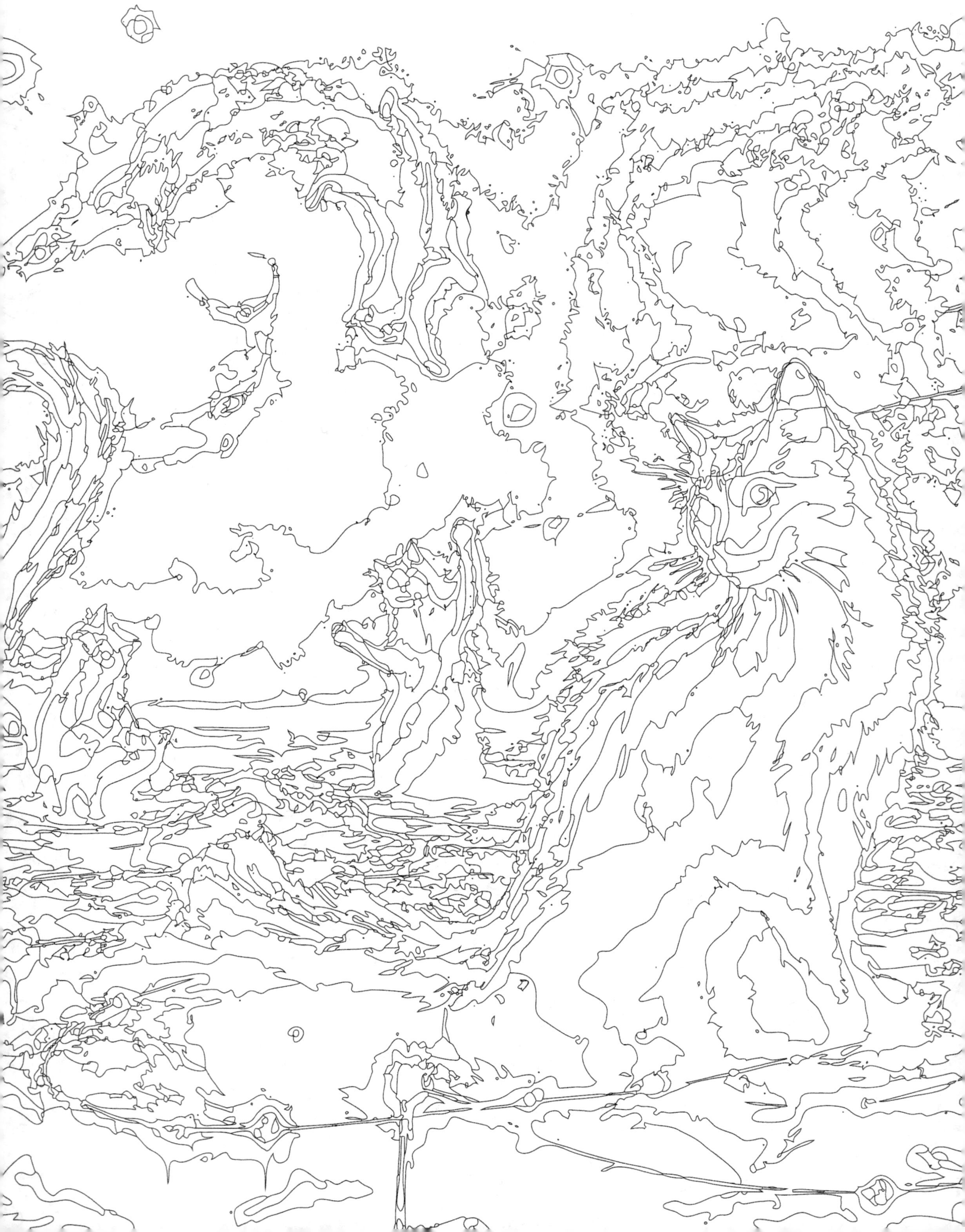

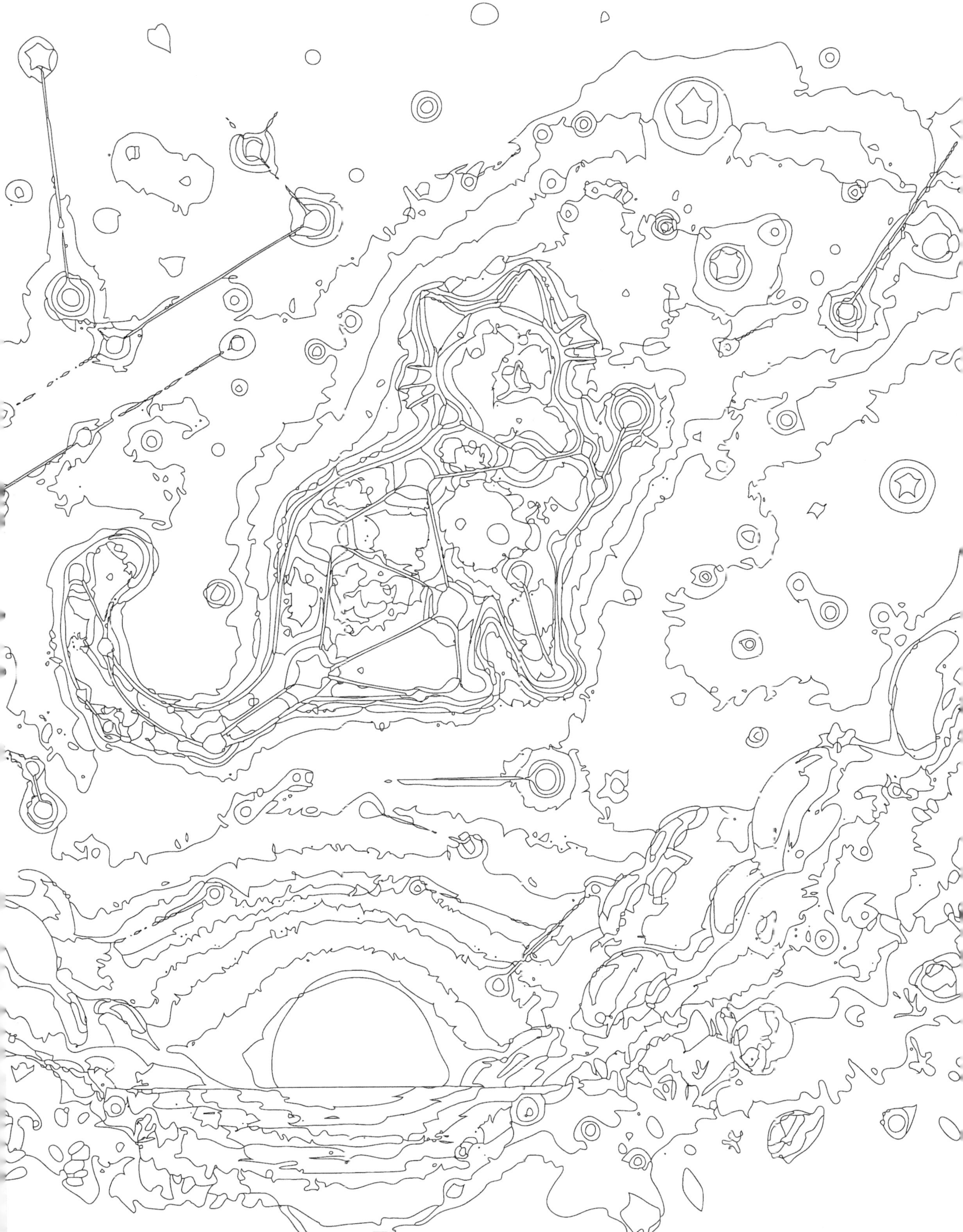

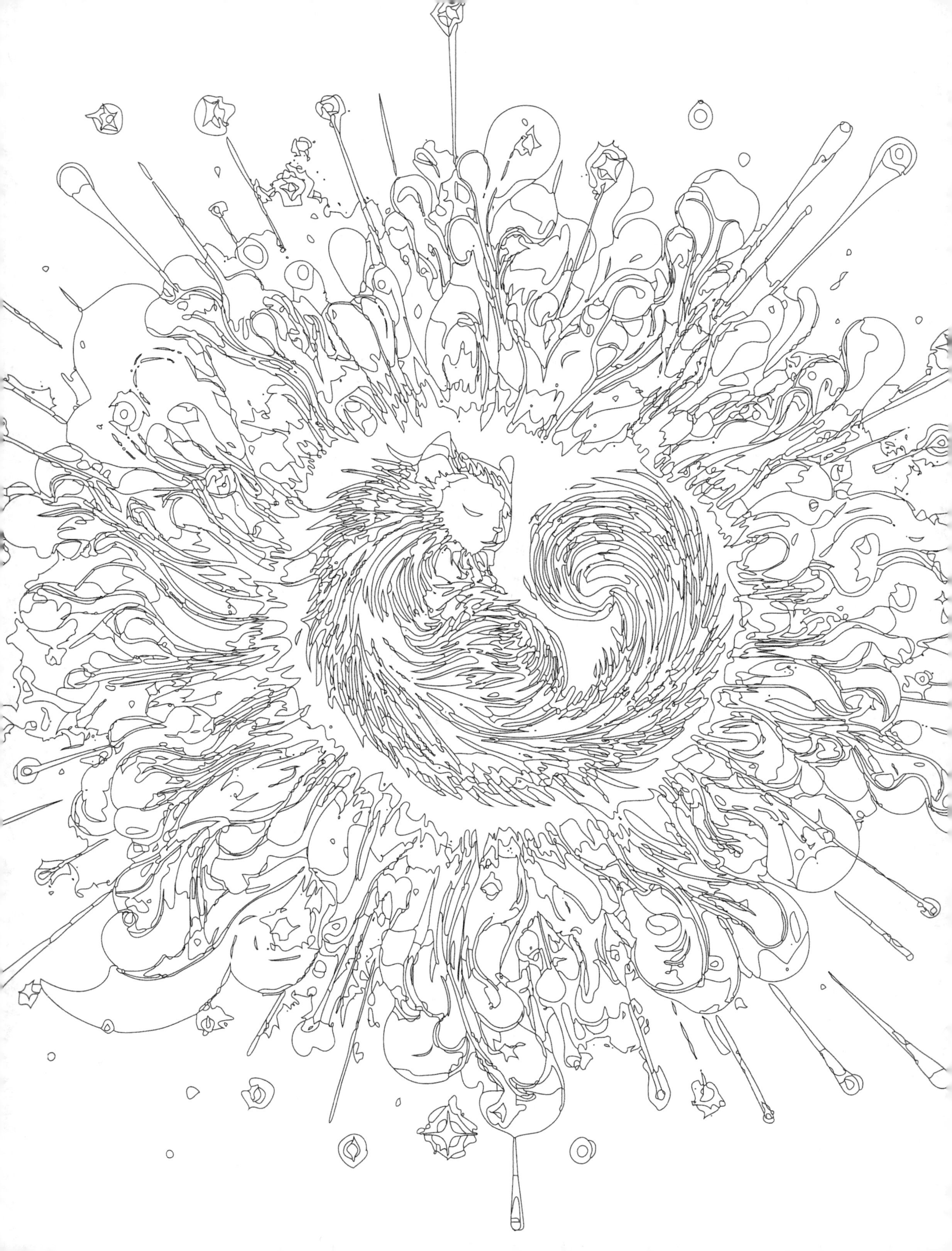

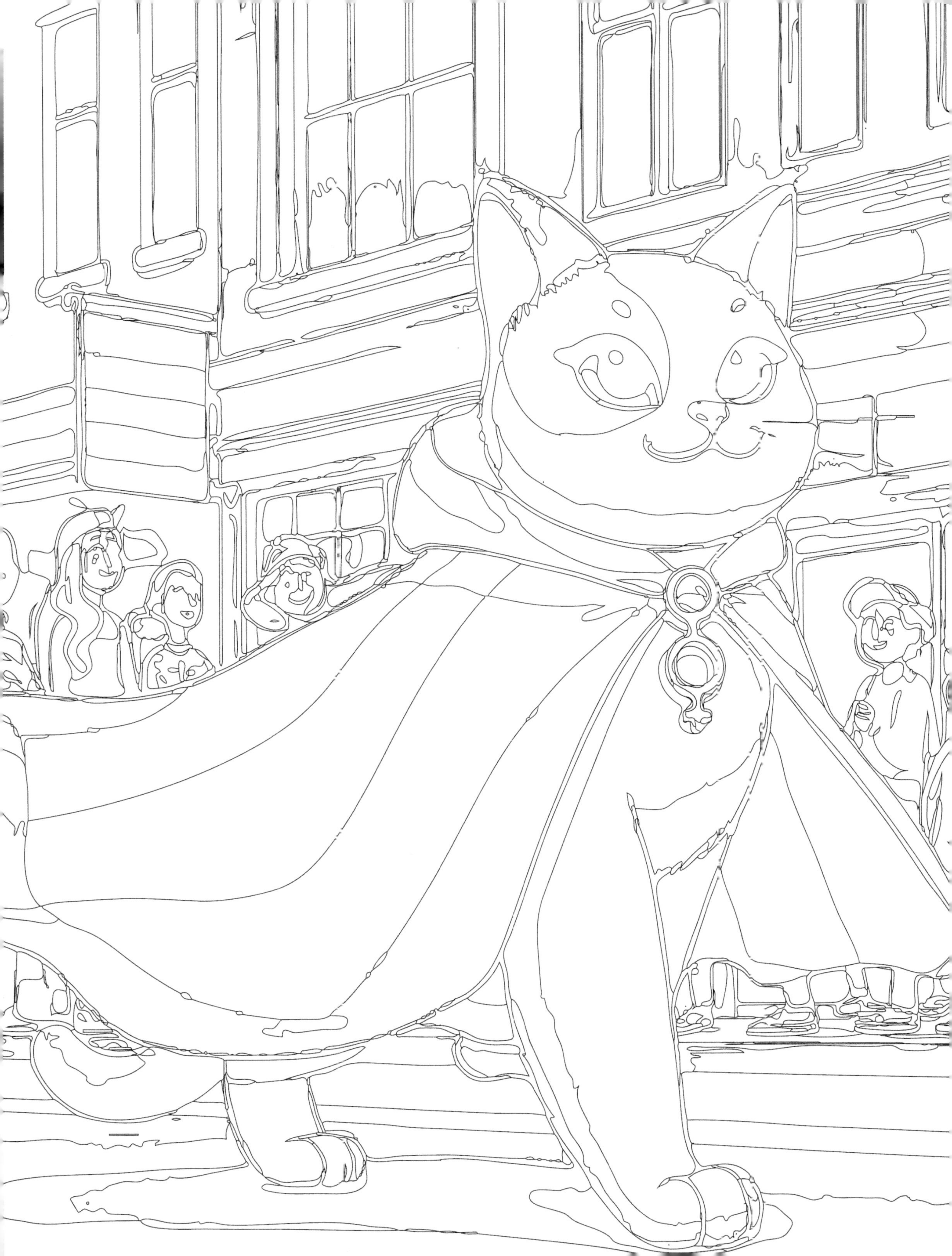

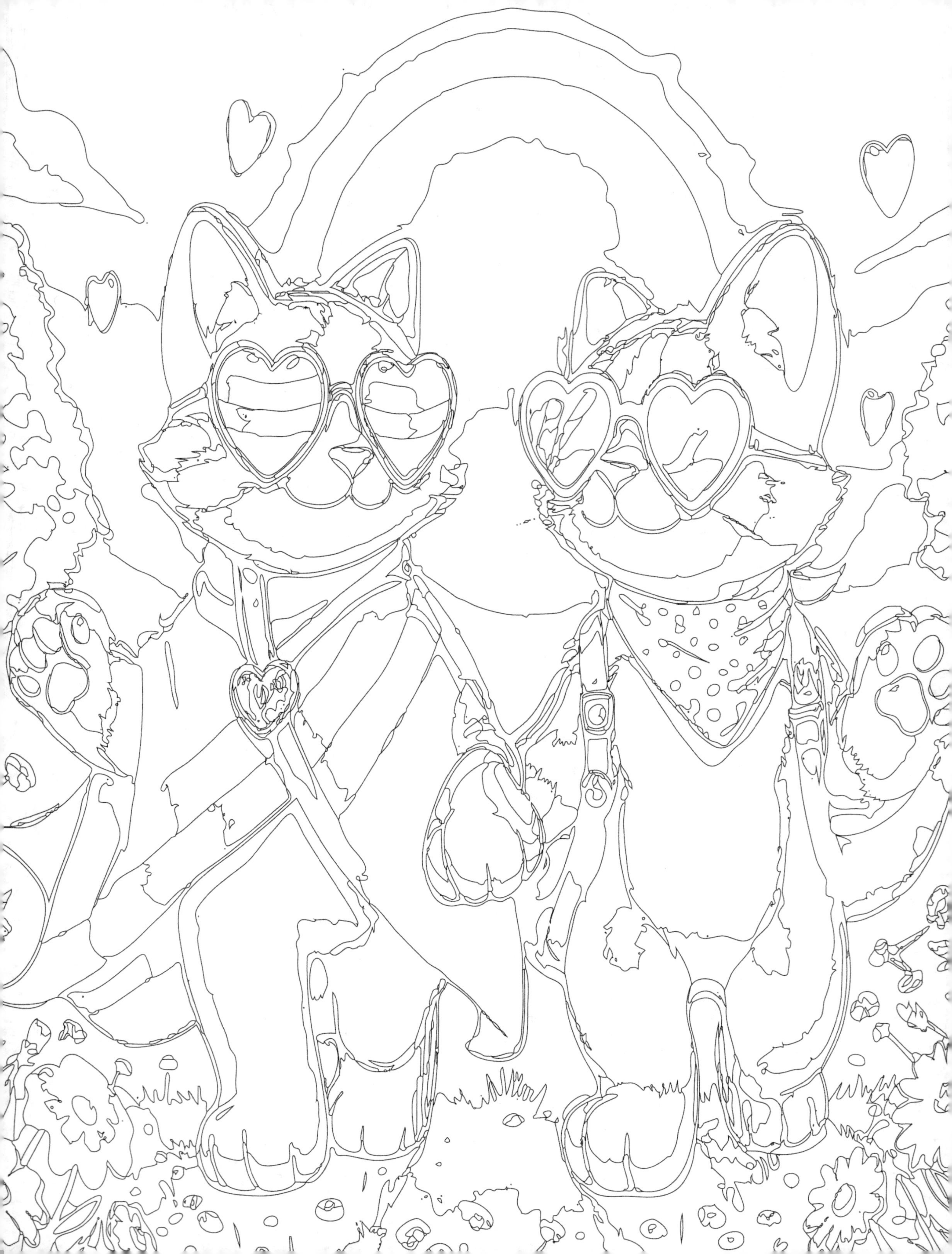

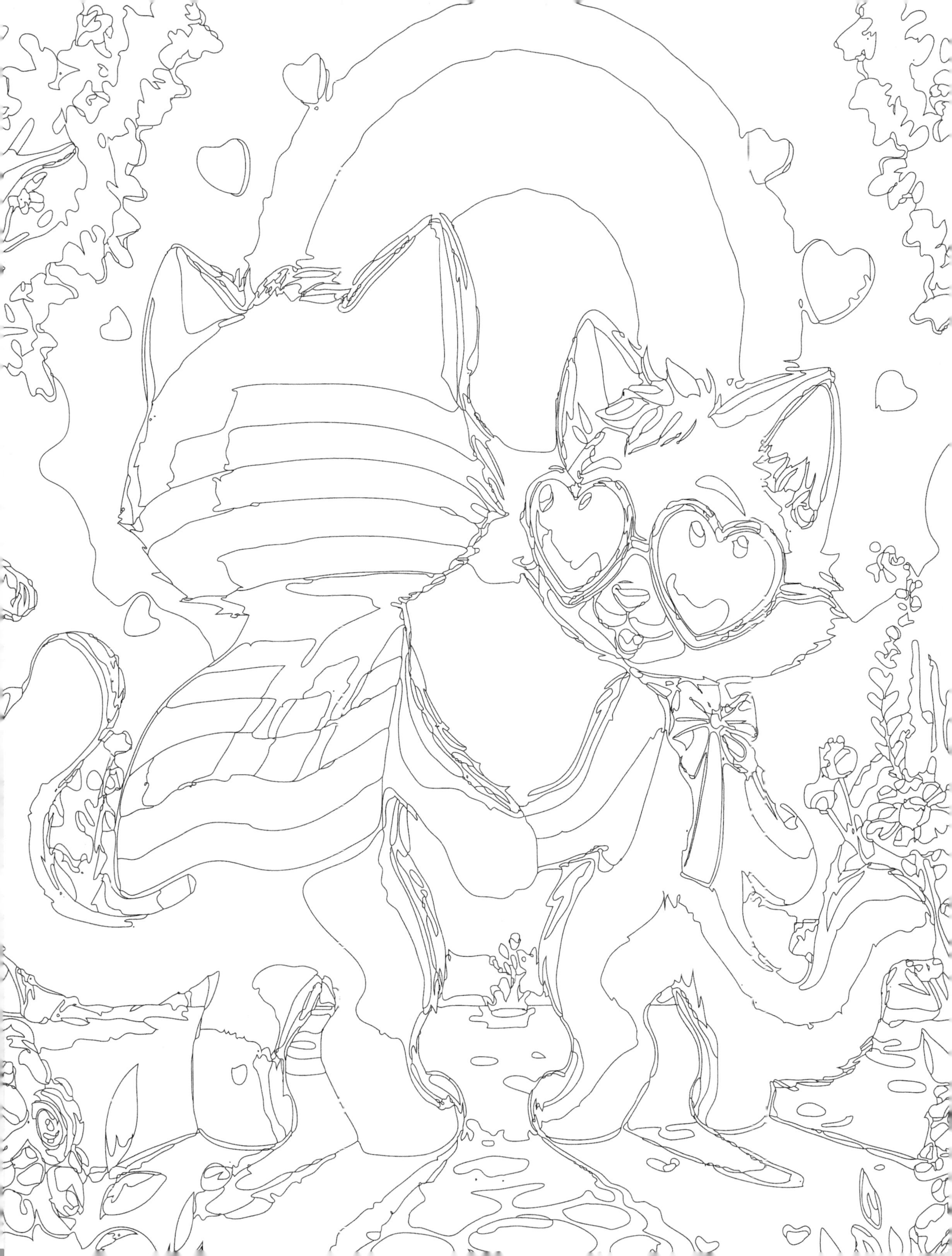

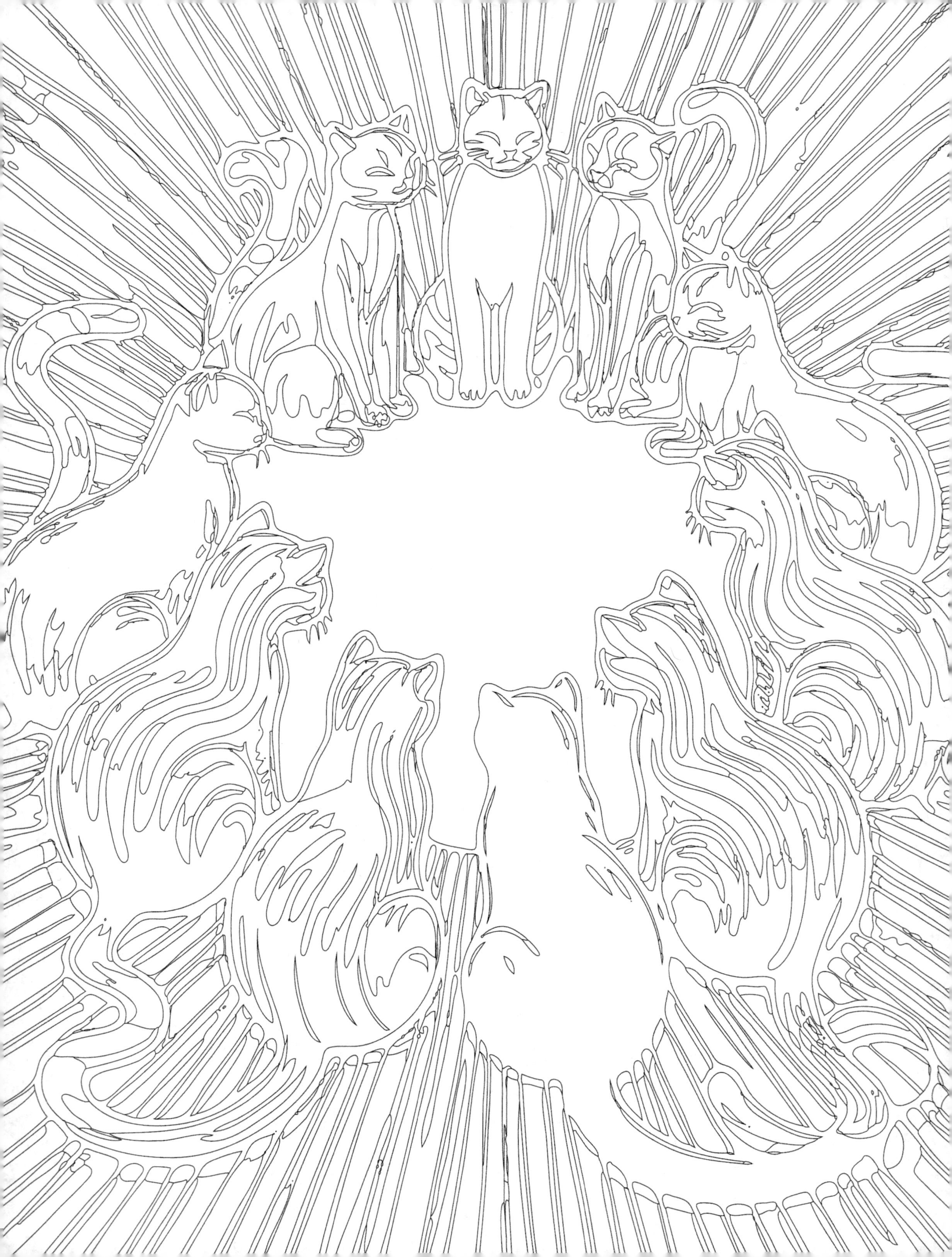

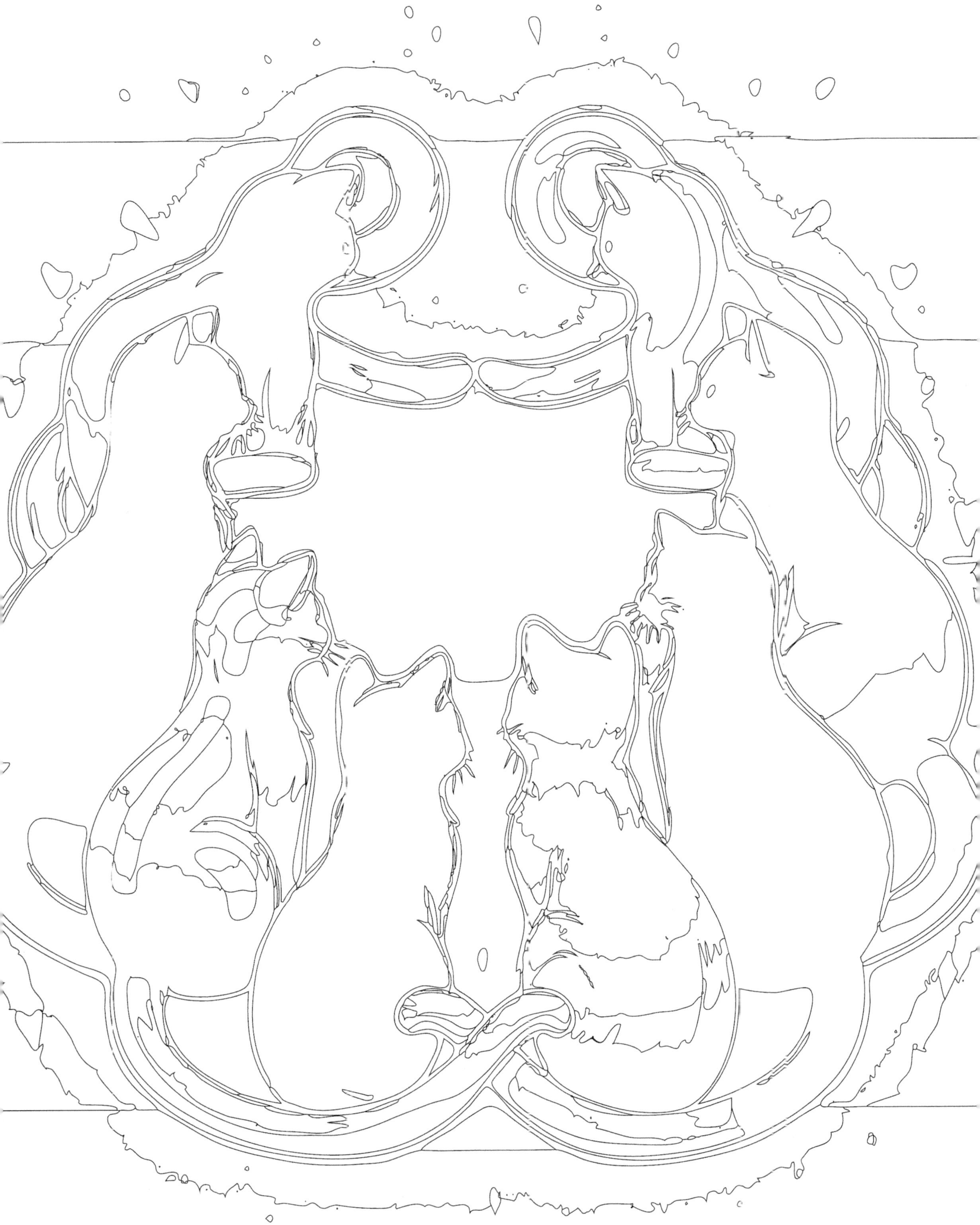

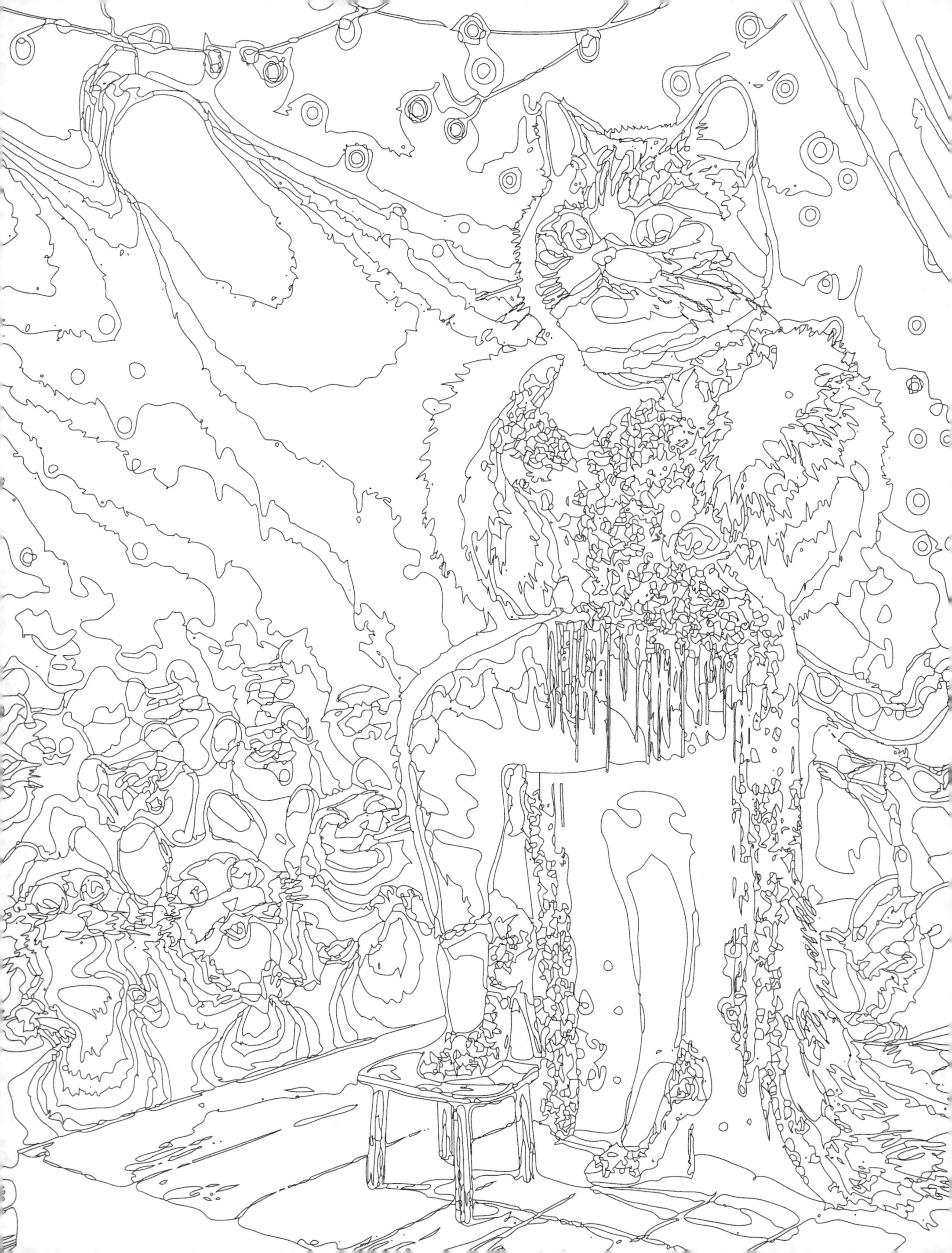

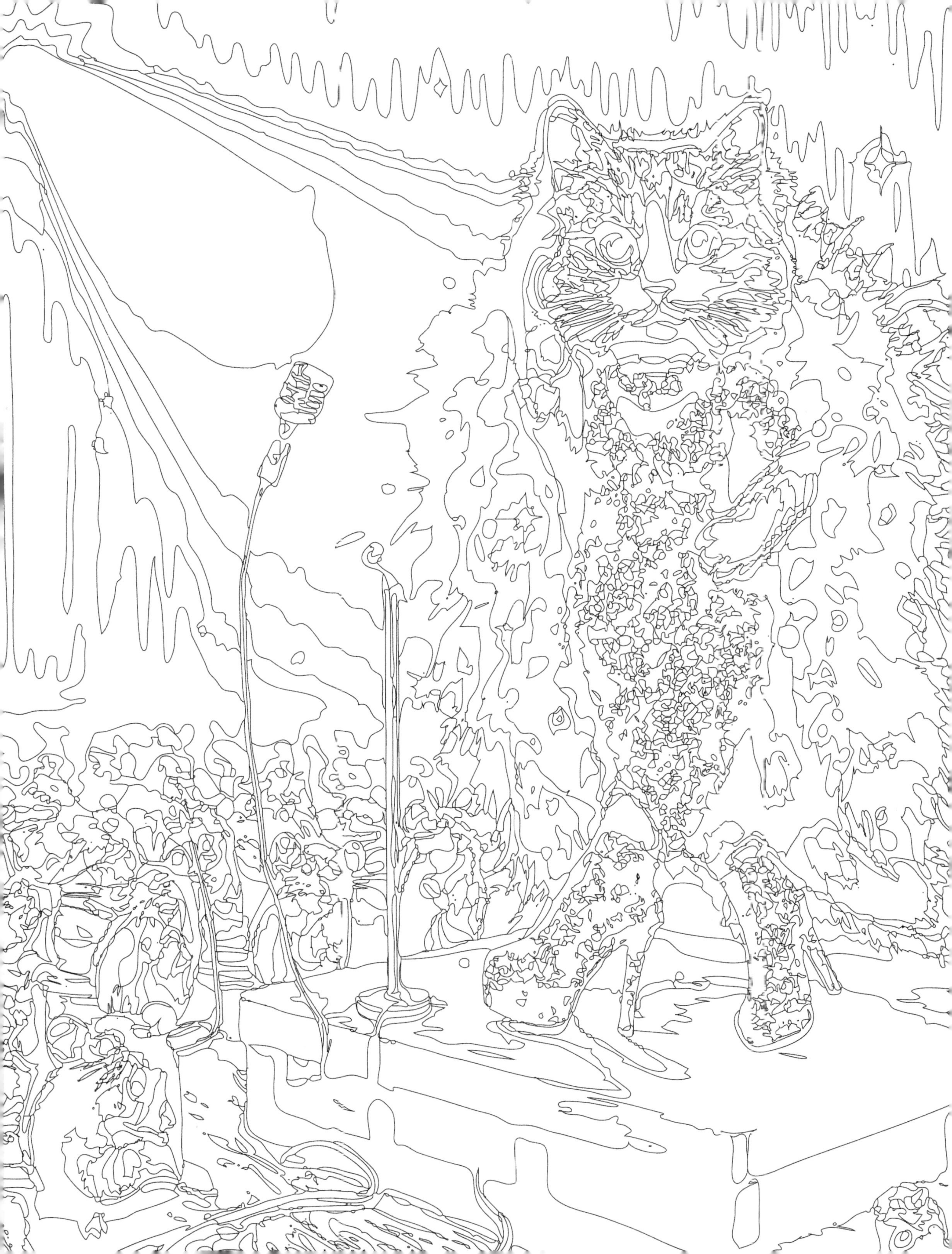

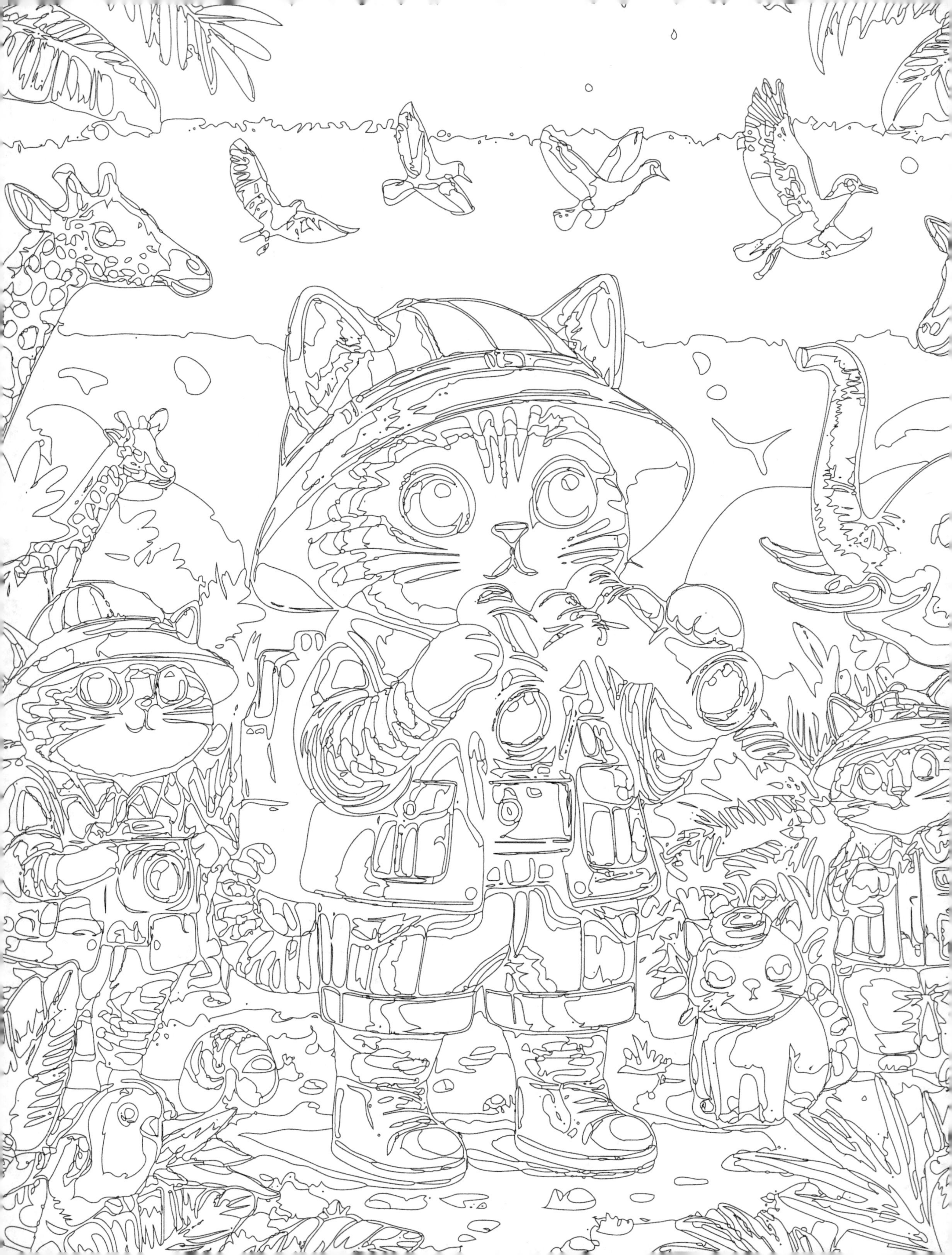

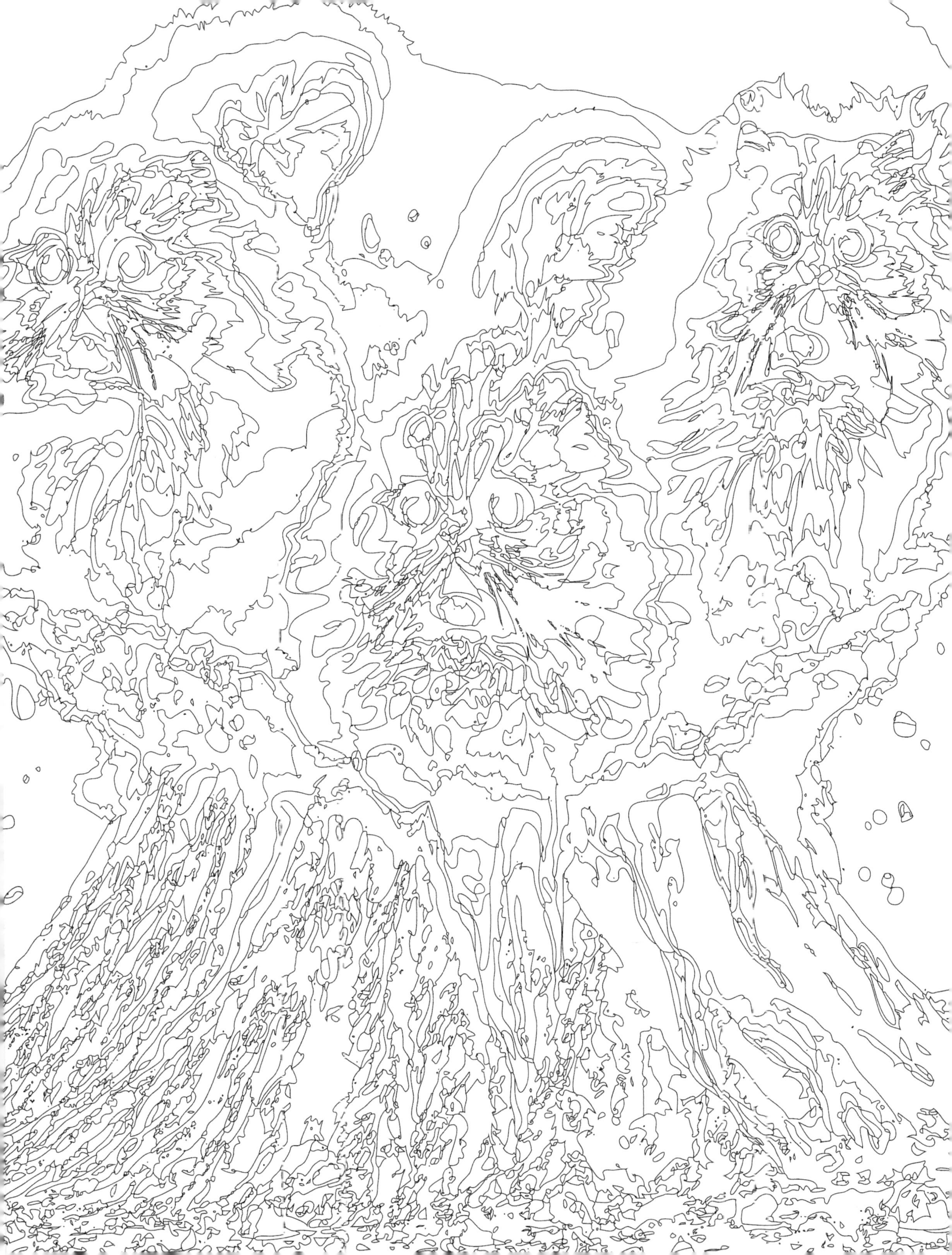

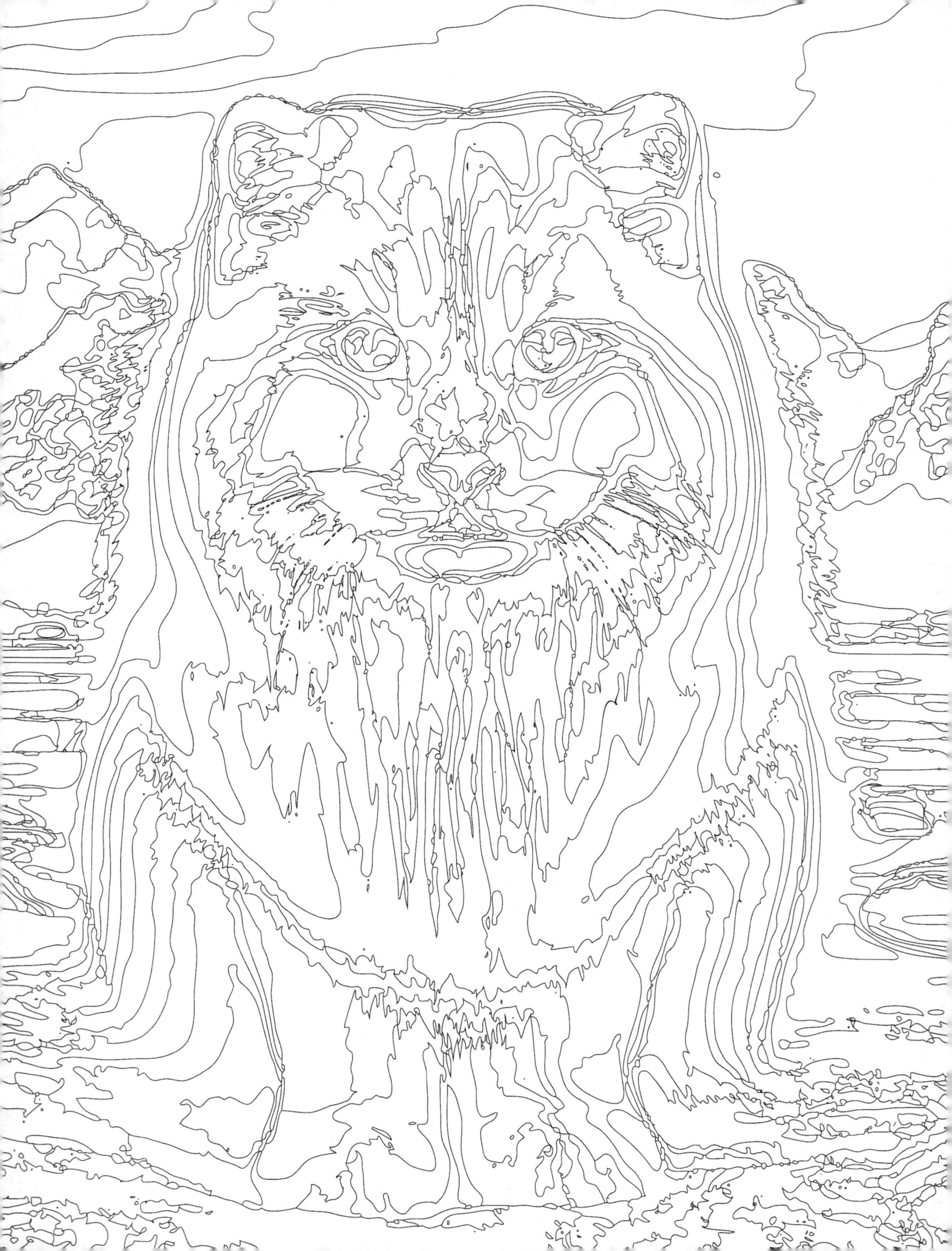

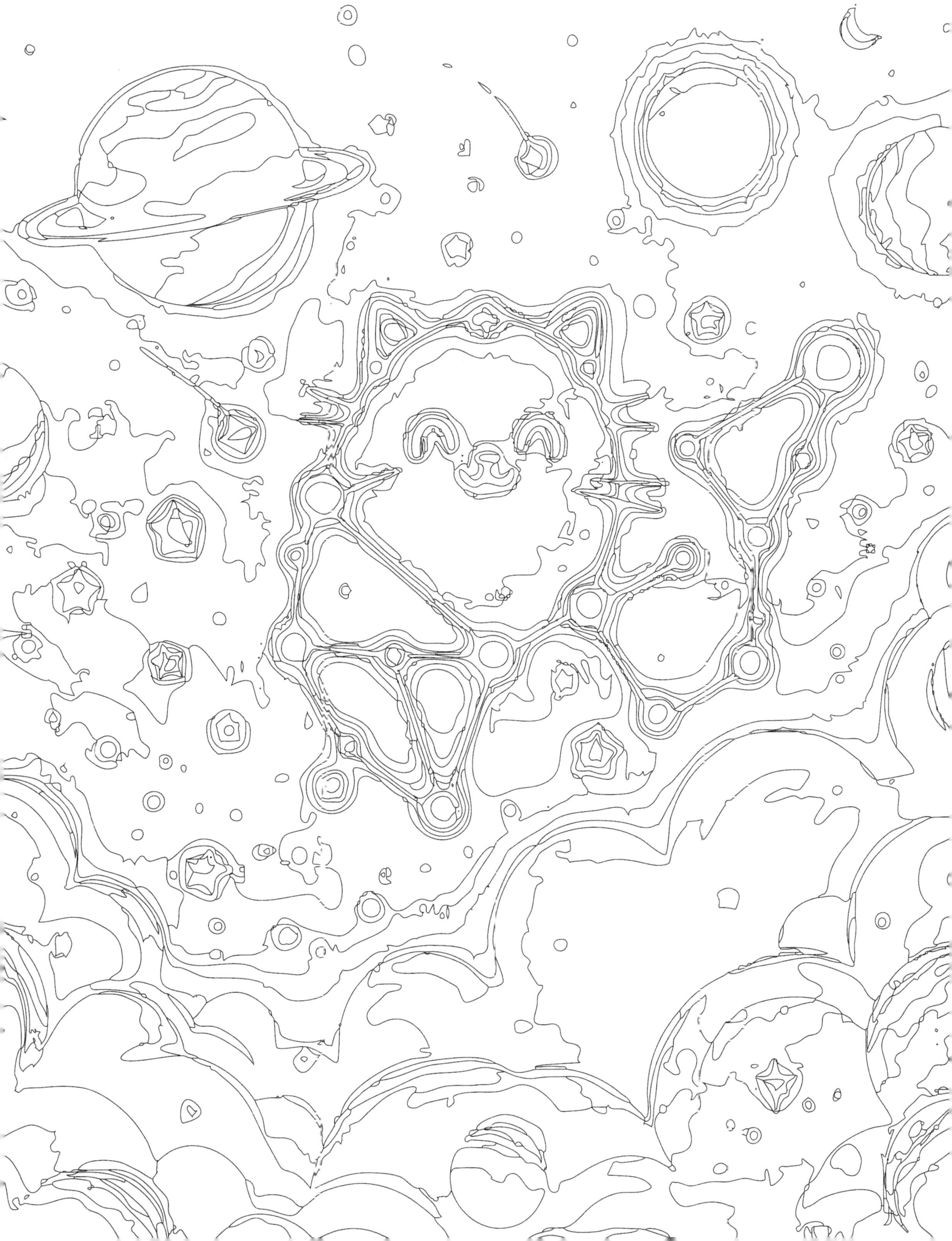

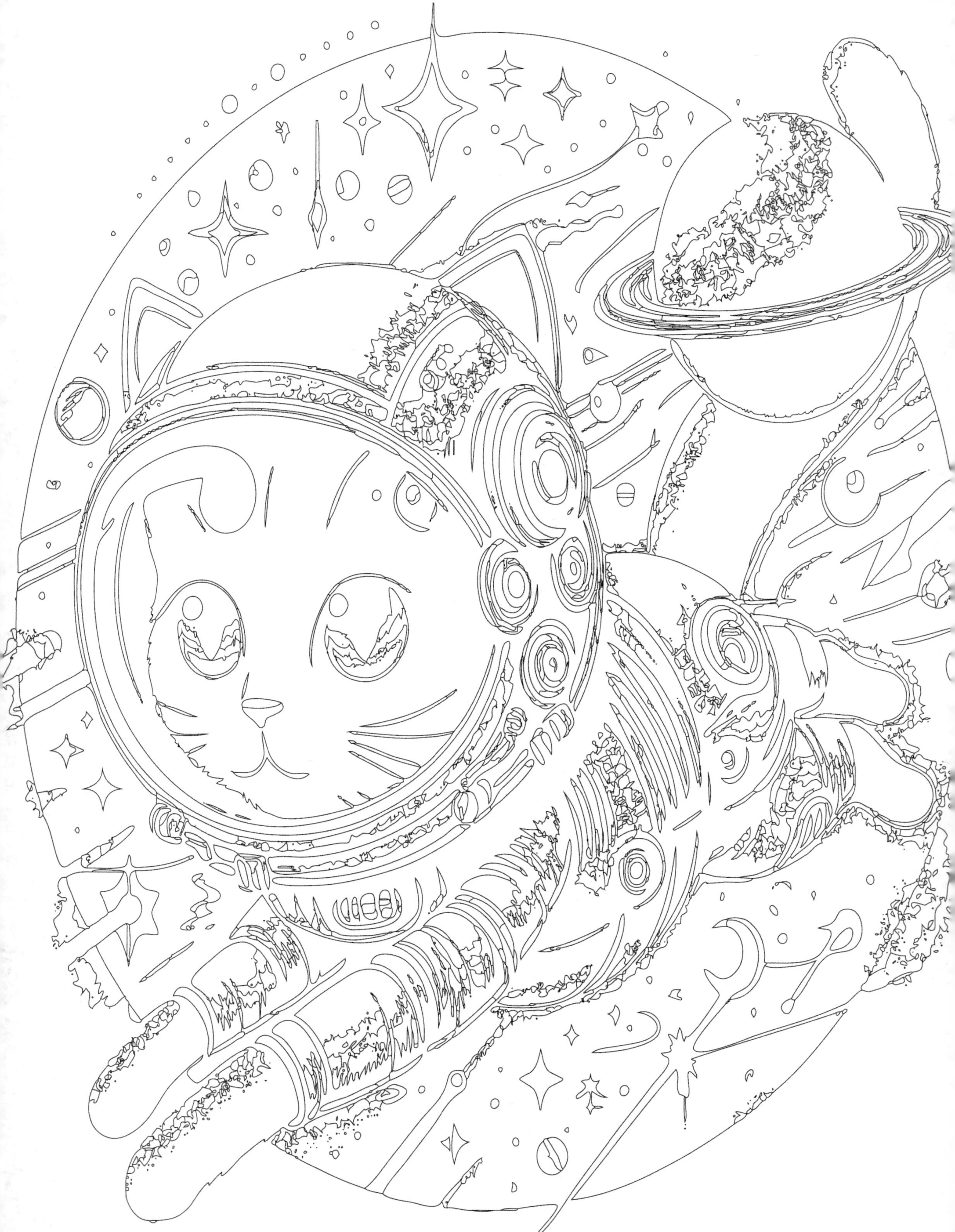

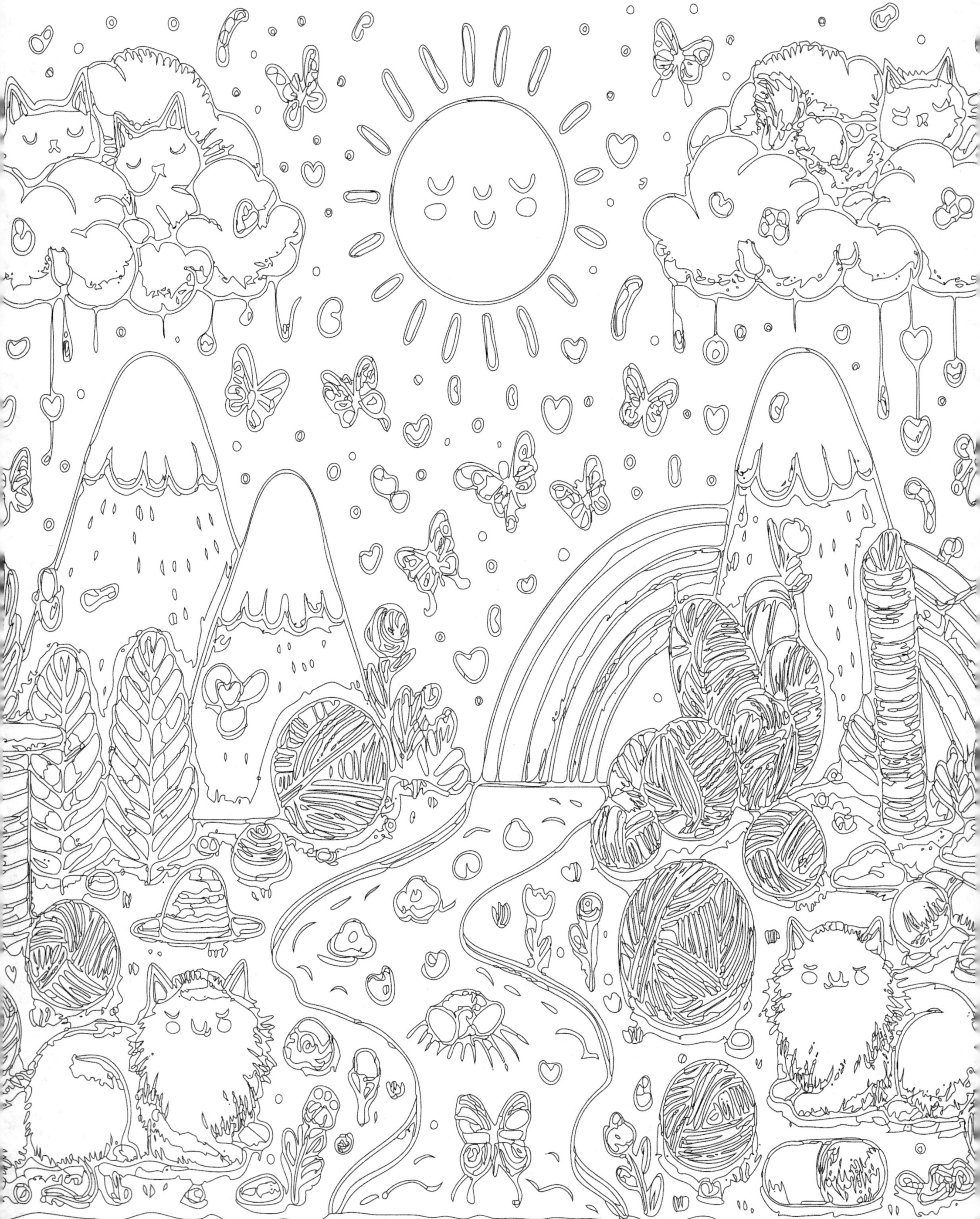

THE COSMIC CAT ADULT COLORING BOOK

100 CATS

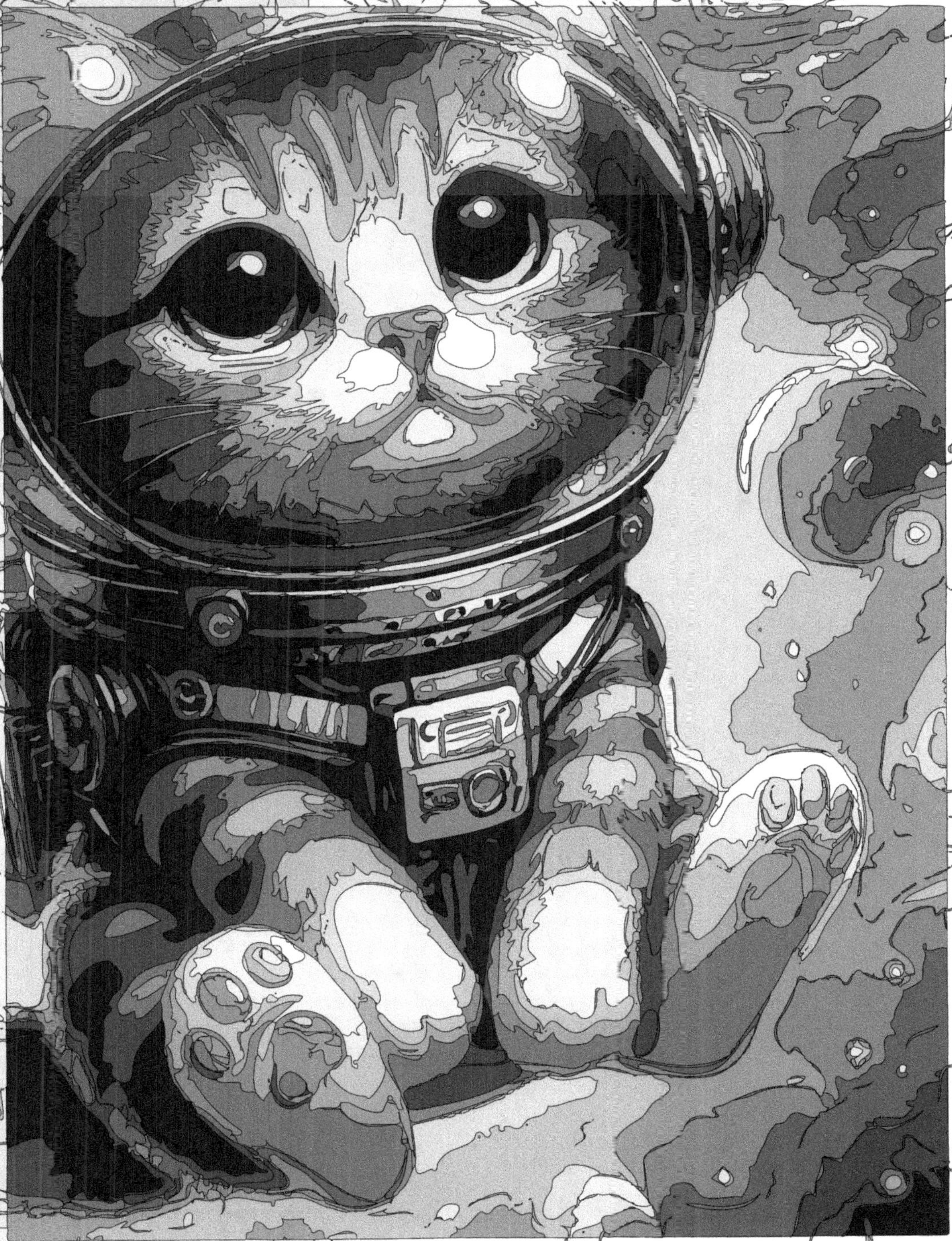

ILLUSTRATED BY
NOVA XERA
A ROOXAA, LLC PRODUCTION

www.ingramcontent.com/pod-product-compliance
Lightning Source LLC
Chambersburg PA
CBHW062114220526
45471CB00010B/3728
9798321642153